STAR!

RICHARD WARREN RAPPAPORT

STAR!

Finding Artistic and Commercial Success
in the New Entertainment Industry

Cover by Elmarie Jara/ABA Publishing.

Printed in the United States of America

17 16 15 14 13   5 4 3 2

Library of Congress Cataloging-in-Publication Data

Rappaport, Richard Warren.
  Star! : finding artistic and commercial success in the new
entertainment industry / Richard Warren Rappaport, American Bar
Association.
     pages cm
  ISBN 978-1-61438-839-5
  1. Performing arts--Law and legislation--United States. 2.
Entertainers--United States--Handbooks, manuals, etc. I. Title.
  KF4290.R37 2012
  790.2023'73--dc23
                         2012045836

Discounts are available for books ordered in bulk. Special consideration is given to state bars, CLE programs, and other bar-related organizations. Inquire at Book Publishing, ABA Publishing, American Bar Association, 321 North Clark Street, Chicago, Illinois 60654-7598.

www.ShopABA.org

All the world's a stage,
And all the men and women merely players;
They have their exits and their entrances . . .

William Shakespeare, *As You Like It*

DEDICATION

To the artistry in all of us, so that we may touch the stars and create something that is original and timeless.

CONTENTS

ABOUT THE AUTHOR

Richard Warren Rappaport is an attorney licensed in Florida, New York, and Washington, DC, with offices in Boca Raton and Miami. He practices in entertainment, arts and sports law domestically and internationally, including motion pictures, television, music, theater, the classical arts, the literary arts, the fine arts, sports, fashion, media, intellectual property, and the Internet. He also practices in media law, communications law, corporate law, and international law and trade,

He is a graduate of Georgetown University Law Center (LLM), the University of Miami School of Law (JD) and Boston University School of Management (BSBA). He is on the Governing Board of the American Bar Association (ABA) Forum on the Entertainment and Sports Industries, and is a co-chair for the forum's annual conferences, "From New York to Hollywood to South Beach: The International Legal Symposium on the World of Music, Film, Television and Sports."

Mr. Rappaport is a former partner at Yoss LLP (2001-11), a past chair of the Florida Bar Entertainment, Arts and Sports Law Section, a former member of its Executive Council, and a past co-chair of its annual Legal Symposium on the World of Music, Film and Television. He is a member of the National Academy of Television Arts & Sciences (The Daytime Emmy Awards), The Academy of

Television Arts & Sciences (The Primetime Emmy Awards), and The Recording Academy (The Grammy Awards). He is "AV" rated by Martindale-Hubbell and has been named many times in *Super Lawyers* magazine, Florida edition, within the field of Entertainment and Sports.

Mr. Rappaport began his career as an attorney in the Cable Television Bureau at The Federal Communications Commission, and also worked as an investigative attorney at the United States International Trade Commission, both in Washington, DC. He then entered private practice in Washington, DC, and later opened offices in New York City, Miami, and Boca Raton.

He has lectured extensively on entertainment law and has authored or co-authored various published articles in that field, including "Inside Hollywood: The Reel Path to Success in the Motion Picture Industry," *Entertainment and Media Law Contract Strategies*, Aspatore Books, Boston, reprinted in the ABA's Forum on the Entertainment and Sports Industries Newsletter.

Mr. Rappaport has spent his life in professional music, and is a BMI-affiliated recording artist, writer, and publisher. His music has been in film, and on television and radio. He has also performed live on television, radio and on stage, and at numerous events in support of the arts, including the Broward Center for the Performing Arts and the Steinway/BMI Music and Arts Showcase.

His soulful composition, *Louisiana Way,* was in the soundtrack of the CBS Television Movie of the Week, *The Madam's Family: The Truth About the Canal Street Brothel*, and was placed in consideration for an Emmy™ nomination for soundtrack source music. His tropical ballad, *Sail Into The Sun,* charted into the Top 20 on the

Friday Morning Quarterback (FMQB) national adult contemporary charts. And his pop classic, *Great Rock 'N' Roll*, which first received airplay in Philadelphia, became the theme song for the television show *Hello Hollywood*, broadcast on WHDT, West Palm Beach, Florida, now on iStudioi.com.

He has produced in film and television and has been an on-air personality, hosting *American Law*, a series of television vignettes on the law, which aired in New York City and Miami. He also co-produced and co-hosted *Hello Hollywood* on television.

Mr. Rappaport made his film debut behind the camera in the documentary motion picture and docu-concert, "Concert," which he directed and also co-produced with Robert Berkowitz and executive producer René Katz. The film was borne out of his live acoustic solo concert and benefit performance in Miami. The goal of the producers was to provide an introspective and reflective story of the genesis of original music, its importance to the creative process and the significance of the message to be delivered. Through the musical performances and interviews in "Concert," art and creativity merge in a portrait of the inspiration that lives within music, the stories behind the songs and the songs behind the stories.

"Concert" premiered at the Ft. Lauderdale International Film Festival at the historic Cinema Paradiso. It also screened at the prestigious Women in Film Independent Film Series in Los Angeles, the ABA's International Legal Symposium on the World of Music, Film, Television and Sports in Miami, Beach, and The Boca Raton Museum of Art. "Concert" had its world premiere as the official opening night film at the acclaimed Doc'Miami International Film Festival.

Mr. Rappaport is active in civic, community and charitable organizations in South Florida, New York, and Los Angeles. He believes in the importance of ongoing discussions on topics and issues facing the entertainment industry today, and supports the film, television, and music industries and the emerging and established creative talent within it.

STAR: Finding Artistic and Commercial Success in the New Entertainment Industry is his first book.

ACKNOWLEDGMENTS

The individuals below provided professional expertise and fascinating insights so that I may share some of their thoughts and comments with you. They are listed in alphabetical order.

James Adler; Carolina Garcia-Aguilera; Amanda Alexandrakis; Steve Alten; Elizabeth Angulo; Joseph Arrington II, Esq.; Dr. Kenneth J. Atchity; Michael Axman, Esq.; Wayne B. Baxley; Bob Berkowitz; Gabe Berman; Todd Brabec, Esq.; John F. Bradley, Esq.; David Brigati; Kate Burgauer; Aaron Carter; Martin Cass, CPA; Arlen Castillo; and Barbie Castro.

Darryl B. Cohen, Esq.; Dr. Andrea Corn; Gregory Curtner, Esq.; Peter Dekom, Esq.; Adriana De Moura; Dixon Q. Dern, Esq.; Marc Durso; Jenna Edwards; Jean Landfair Enright; Gina Franano; Robin Abramovitz Goldberg; Emily P. Graham, Esq.; Ingrid Hoffman; and Dr. James Huysman.

Coach Mike Jarvis; Celeste Jones; Maxim Kantor; René Katz; Madeleine Kirsh; Jeffrey L. Klein; Mark W. Koch; Kimberly D. Kolback, Esq.; Katherine T. Koonce; Michael S. Leone, CPA; Paul LiCalsi, Esq.; and Daniel de Liege.

Diana Lozano; Jan Michael Morris, Esq.; Lauren Morris; Lazaro Mur, Esq.; Garry O'Donnell, Esq.; Victoria Ann Parker; Lynn Parks; the late Mark Poncy; Pat Quinn; Regina Rachael; George Rios; Henry Root, Esq.; Susan Schaefer, Esq.; Fred A. Schwartz, Esq.; and Joseph Serling, Esq.

Frannie Sheridan; Sommore; Maryann Ridini Spencer; Gregory St. John III, Esq.; George N. Stein, Esq.; Tim Warnock, Esq.; Howard J. Wiener, Esq.; Richard Willis Jr.; and Alexandria Xiaoli Zheng.

The contributions of James Adler, Maxim Kantor, Lynn Parks, Pat Quinn, and Richard Willis Jr., were based on interviews conducted by the author for iStudioi.com.

SPECIAL THANKS

I would like to thank Timothy D. Brandhorst, Director of New Product Development, ABA Publishing, for his guidance and assistance in having this book published.

I would also like to thank my editor, Kate Burgauer, President of Compass Rose Creative Services, for her editorial assistance with the manuscript, and CheckPROZ, LLC, for its copyediting services.

I would like to thank Richard G. Paszkiet, Director of Entity Book Publishing, ABA Book Publishing, Teresa Ucok, Forum Manager, the ABA Forum on the Entertainment and Sports Industries, Robert G. Pimm, Book Publishing Chair of the Forum, and Kimberly D. Kolback, Esq., for their thoughtful and constructive suggestions during the writing of the manuscript.

And my special thanks go to film and television producer, broadcaster, and on-air personality René Katz for her assistance with this book, my motion picture "Concert," about the artistry of music, and my work as an attorney and artist in this fascinating world of the entertainment industry.

FOREWORD

The world of entertainment is a fascinating one.

On any given day, new artistic content is being created, and in many instances the artist is guided by pure talent and imagination. He or she may not have any thought of personal or financial gain, but may simply desire to create something new and to present original and dynamic content for all of us to enjoy.

As attorneys, we are sometimes imbued with the responsibility to represent such artists and to act as advisors, providing our guidance, advice, and counsel. In this regard, as with all clients, we have a legal, ethical, and moral obligation to provide that service to the best of our abilities.

In the world of entertainment law, what makes our work unique is having the rare opportunity to represent that aspiring artist who has a dream of finding success in the entertainment industry and who is completely dedicated to fulfilling that dream.

In this sense, we may find ourselves not only conveying legal advice to the artist as a client, but also rendering an opinion on whether the quality of the content as presented conforms to current standards and practices within the entertainment industry.

In essence, this book seeks to describe the artist's path in the climb toward artistic, professional, and commercial success. It addresses the role of the artist's team, with the entertainment lawyer at the forefront, acting as a trusted advisor, facilitator, colleague, and friend to help make the dream a reality.

It has been said that the journey toward a goal is just as important as the achievement of the goal itself. In the entertainment industry that is very true, for during this journey the artist is never alone. The team must always be there, by the artist's side, providing all of the advice and counsel that is necessary for success.

Welcome to the world of the new entertainment industry. I hope you enjoy the book; let's begin the journey.

—*Fred A. Schwartz, Esq., Boca Raton and New York City*

INTRODUCTION

---

*To be a Star is about more than just a title and com-
merical success. It is about artistry, creativity, vision,
commitment to the arts, responsibility toward others,
mentoring the next generation of artists, and involvement in education, philanthropy and charitable and
civic involvement. Once you have attained the above,
you are a Star.*

Richard Warren Rappaport

This book is about your creative star and finding artistic and commercial success in the new entertainment industry.

It is written for anyone who is involved in the industry and the
world of motion pictures, television, music, the literary arts, fashion and modeling, the visual arts and fine arts, or any other aspect
of the creative arts.

Covering all major genres of entertainment, this book provides
a unique overview of the artistic, business, and legal aspects of the
industry. To accomplish this, it provides in-depth interviews with
some of the most prominent attorneys in the country practicing

in entertainment law, including entertainment-related transactions and litigation, corporate law, tax law, trust and estate law, accounting, and wealth management and preservation. It also provides interviews of experienced industry professionals who are producers, actors, screenwriters, novelists, musicians, vocalists, songwriters, choreographers, comedians, photographers, visual artists, personalities, hosts and spokespersons, literary managers, talent managers, acting coaches, former agents, editors, specialists in marketing and promotion, publicists, motivational psychologists, and others in the world of entertainment.

Taken together, the interviews provide a sense of the intricate texture and fascinating mosaic that constitutes the entertainment industry as seen by Hollywood insiders, who discuss the delicate balance between artistry and commercialism on the path to success.

The book is organized into seven chapters. Chapter One presents the artistry of the entertainment industry in all its forms. Chapter Two discusses the commercial structure of that industry, describing how artistry and business meet and sometimes collide. Chapter Three introduces the all-important team often led by the entertainment attorney. The team also includes the talent manager, the literary manager and writing coach, the agent, the editor, the producer, and the publicist. This powerful and experienced group of professionals is vitally important to the artist's career as the artist and team work closely together on the path toward the achievement of artistic and commercial success.

Chapter Four discusses the critical professional introduction of the artist to the industry, and the type of legal entity to utilize in the quest for success. Chapter Five addresses that all-important development deal that may make or break an artist's career, as well as the opportunities that arise within the industry from such deals. Also discussed are opportunities for those artists who are determined to start their own companies and blaze a new independent path for their artistry through business, marketing, and promotion within the new industry paradigm.

Chapter Six salutes the attainment of artistic and commercial success within the industry, as the artist develops new professional relationships and seeks to manage and preserve wealth. Chapter Seven analyzes the inevitable results of such success and the responsibilities that come with it, including the need for artistic leadership, an understanding of the incredible power of celebrity, the importance of education and mentoring, and involvement in charitable and civic affairs.

Each chapter covers a particular aspect of the industry and opens with "The Basics," a preview of what is to be addressed in that chapter. It is followed by "Why This Chapter Is Important to You," which discusses the relevance of the chapter to the entertainment industry and provides a bullet-point overview of film, television, music, literary arts, fashion and modeling, and visual and fine arts.

The content of each chapter is also divided into topical subsections, and each subsection has a summary, or "Instant Replay," prior to the next subsection. "Counselors, Approach the Bench" speaks to the important role played by the entertainment attorney on the artist's behalf in the metaphorical "Court of Artistic Opinion." And beginning in Chapter Three, "Team Huddle" gives an overview of the general responsibilities of the team members as they guide the artist through the maze of the industry.

"And It's a Wrap" is presented toward the end of each chapter and provides some thoughts for consideration as well as specific suggestions for the development of particular career paths, once again with a bullet-point industry overview. "Lights, Camera, Action!" provides a glimpse of the chapter ahead and is followed by a story inspired by an individual who sought and found artistic and commercial success in the new entertainment industry.

This book is for all those who work in the world of entertainment, including producers, directors, cinematographers, agents, actors, screenwriters, novelists, musicians, vocalists, songwriters, composers, personalities, hosts, spokespersons, models, visual artists, personal managers, business managers, literary managers, writing coaches, editors, publicists, and anyone who has a serious artistic and professional interest in the industry.

It is also for attorneys practicing in the entertainment industry—including entertainment, arts, and sports law; media law; Internet law; communications law; intellectual property law; and corporate and international law—who are involved in advising clients in the expanding world of entertainment, both domestically and internationally.

This book is for undergraduate, graduate, or law students who wish to develop a general knowledge of the industry from the perspective of those who are actively engaged in it.

In essence, if you wish to understand the fascinating world of the new entertainment industry, this book is for you.

AUTHOR'S NOTE

The opinions expressed in this book are solely those of the author and/or the respective contributors. As such, this book is not intended to replace legal or business advice or knowledge provided by an attorney or other industry professional.

It is recommended that the reader utilize the services of a qualified and experienced attorney in entertainment, arts, and sports law and/or any other relevant industry professional prior to making legal and business decisions that may affect his or her career.

All trademarks, service marks, or registered marks presented in this book are the property of their respective owners. Any characters that may be portrayed in this book are fictitious, and any similarity to the name, character, likeness, or history of any person is coincidental and unintentional.

PRELUDE

YOU, THE ARTIST:
REACHING FOR THE DREAM

New York nights, New York lights and New York love
Let's take a ride on a midnight drive
Wake up to the sun.

Richard Warren Rappaport,
"New York Nights," from the motion picture
soundtrack of *Concert*

YOU, THE ARTIST

Artistry has a beginning. But it never really has an end. It lives within us and is a part of our being. That is the very nature of creativity and a reflection of your creative star, which lies on the horizon, waiting to be discovered.

This book is about you, the artist, and all those around you who will help make your dream come true. It is about finding artistic and professional success in the entertainment industry, or "the industry," as we often call it.

For those of us who work in the industry and the world of entertainment, we are profoundly affected by the attraction it brings, its magical and sometimes mystical aura and its larger than life reputation. And you exist as an artist within it.

Your artistry is limited only by your imagination and drive. Your talent defines itself. It cannot be measured quantitatively, but only qualitatively, as you develop, nurture, and express your art.

And who are you as the artist? You may be an actor or actress, defining a role you create or are given. You may be a vocalist, guitarist, drummer, pianist/keyboardist, flutist, or other musician, composing and performing your own music or interpreting and stylizing the works of others. Or you may have been trained as a visual artist, giving the world a glimpse of your vision of it. Or perhaps you are a performer in a ballet or modern dance company. Or maybe you are an author, screenwriter, or poet, speaking to your audience in your individual, introspective way. Or you are living your dream as a producer or director, bringing that next great motion picture, television series, or Broadway play to life.

You are the artist. And your art is your gift to yourself and the world. We honor you, your work, and your dedication to artistic success.

This book is about finding that path to success in the new entertainment industry and the journey that takes you there. It is about achieving excellence in your artistic endeavors and reaching new horizons, creating new boundaries, and sharing your talents with the world in an industry that is unique.

And why do you do it? It is because of your desire to make an artistic mark upon the world.

For those artists who are reaching for the dream, I dedicate this book to you.

—*Richard Warren Rappaport, Boca Raton, Miami, New York and Washington, DC*

ONE

THE ARTISTRY OF THE ENTERTAINMENT INDUSTRY

Bless your feet, they'll take you places
When your thumb runs outta' gas
Cross your heart and pray to Jesus
That your broken back might last
In this damn forsaken parish
Where you might just rot away
New Orleans sun is shinin' down Louisiana Way.

Richard Warren Rappaport, "Louisiana Way," from the motion picture soundtrack of *Concert* and *The Madam's Family: The Truth about the Canal Street Brothel*

THE BASICS

This chapter is about the artistry of the entertainment industry, your work within the world of that artistry, and your creativity and originality in all its forms and genres.

Your commitment to your artistic goals is discussed, including the inspiration to reach for excellence in your work, the path to artistic success, the need to artistically express yourself, and the challenges inherent in creating great art. Also addressed are the ways in which life is expressed through art, how inspiration fosters imagination, the personal satisfaction of the artist in his or her work, the importance of timing in the creation of art, and the relevance of one's artistic roots.

The following topics are analyzed: originality of an artistic concept, passion for one's work, art that speaks to others, creativity from within, and artistic perseverance and discovery in the pursuit of artistic dreams. Lastly, the resilience of the human spirit in art is discussed, including stories that exist within art, the message that art gives us, and the mythology of storytelling and artistic success.

WHY THIS CHAPTER IS IMPORTANT TO YOU

The artistry of the entertainment industry touches every aspect of creativity within the arts.

FILM

* ★ The motion picture industry lives and breathes within the world of creativity. To find success, you must understand the importance of being creative. Producers, directors, screenwriters, actors, and all others involved in film expect to work in that environment. So should you.

* ★ Agents, talent managers, literary managers, and entertainment attorneys also understand the very nature of creativity. In essence, practically all decisions that relate to a motion picture project, from its inception to

completion, are predicated upon the creative quality of that project.

TELEVISION

★ The television networks are always looking for original and creative programming to supplement their schedules and attract a larger audience. Creativity has a home in television, whether you are a director, writer, actor, spokesperson, or network or marketing executive.

★ To be successful in this industry is to be creative. If you work in any capacity within broadcast television, cable television, or satellite-delivered programming, you must think creatively. The success of your career may depend on it.

MUSIC

★ The music industry understands, seeks out, and nurtures creativity. Producers, composers, lyricists, vocalists, musicians, arrangers, and company executives look for the next great star to be born.

★ You must think creatively and be original. The industry demands it.

THE LITERARY ARTS

★ Every publisher in the literary arts is looking for the next best-selling novel, and every author wants to be the one who writes it. Perhaps it will be you.

★ This industry is based upon the creativity, imagination, and talent of its writers and the foresight of traditional publishers, independent publishers, and self-publishers. To enter this world, your writing must be original, creative, and outstanding.

FASHION AND MODELING

★ Avant-garde style, haute couture, and that next great face are what fashion and modeling are all about.

★ In this world, originality and creativity are the first and last word, because the fashion and modeling industries look toward the future, and sometimes the past, to define today's cutting-edge look and style. Are you the next great designer or model to grace the runways across Europe, Asia, and the United States? To get there, you must be creative and original.

THE VISUAL ARTS AND FINE ARTS

★ Visual artists thrive in the world of the fine arts and speak to us through their works. They provide a glimpse of an introspective world through their creative eyes and minds. All great visual artists share a common denominator: creativity and originality. So must you.

★ Gallerists appreciate creativity and originality in the visual arts. They provide the opportunity for an unknown artist to be introduced to the world and for great artists to continue to impress us with their works.

Though it is the artist who creates the work, it is the gallerist who opens the door to artistic success and fame. If your works are expressive, original, and creative, there is a gallerist waiting to exhibit those works.

— THE COURT OF ARTISTIC OPINION —
"COUNSELORS, APPROACH THE BENCH"

Imagine yourself as the artist in the hallway outside the doors of the Court of Artistic Opinion.

Although you crack one of the doors open and peer in, the courtroom is empty and the lights are low. No one has arrived. This is because your creative works have not yet found a commercial outlet. But soon that will change. And once it does, everything will change for you, as the world learns of the artistry of your works.

Your creativity lives within the entertainment industry, just as the entertainment industry lives for creativity. It is the reason for the industry's very existence.

Bring your art to the world!

A STATE OF ART

Creativity is not only a state of mind, but a state of art. To be expressive is to be a creative person in any genre and endeavor. It is that creativity that will permit you to grow as an individual.

All the while, the goal should be to pursue your art and always be true to it.

YOUR GOAL AS AN ARTIST: BELIEVE IN YOUR WORK

Your goal as an artist is to pursue your art to the best of your abilities, setting the highest standards possible in order to achieve excellence.

In essence, it all begins with you.

Former Putnam and HarperCollins author Carolina Garcia-Aguilera is a renowned writer who created the Lupe Solano book series, as well as *One Hot Summer,* which became a Lifetime Television movie. She was also the recipient of the prestigious Shamus Award for her book *Havana Heat.*

Carolina comments on the need to believe in your work. "Publishers want the next great story, but when you give them an original concept, they may initially be hesitant to take the financial or creative risks that are necessary. So you must believe in your work. And you must know your topic." And Carolina adds, "If you are serious about writing, the one thing you should always remember about mindset is not to give up under any circumstances."

In essence, understand your art. That's a great start.

Hollywood film and television producer, literary manager, and writing coach Dr. Kenneth (Ken) J. Atchity, Chairman of Atchity Entertainment International, Inc., The Writer's Lifeline, Inc., and Story Merchant, talks about that type of mindset in the world of writing, the steep but rewarding climb to the top within the industry, and the importance of challenging oneself on a continual basis. "The ideal writer is the one who says, 'there's no end to better,' and who realizes he or she is blessed with a career that allows for continued development as long as the writer lives and writes."

Thus, you must believe in your work and continue to develop

it, making it better as you go along. Your talent as an artist is what will permit you to stand out in the creation of your art, regardless of its genre.

THE CREATIVE NATURE OF YOUR ART

Are you original and creative? Those qualities will distinguish you as an artist.

Diana Lozano, the creator and artistic director of Circ X, a modern-dance theater company, states that the concept of art in performance is very clear. "For me, it's about connection. They say that art is, after all, a universal language. It's in that space between the spectator and the artistic work that magic and love happens. I wish I could live there forever."

Diana finds she is at peace with her art. "Nothing compares to the exhilaration I get from being on stage and performing. I will prepare for weeks and months, rehearsing and creating, all for the next time I can be there in that space where I connect, if even for just a moment."

Always permit your originality and creativity to thrive. Strive to be the best you can be.

INSPIRATION IN YOUR ART

Inspiration in art is crucial to artistic success. Recording artist, actor, and producer Aaron Carter states, "As an artist, my biggest inspirations are my fans and life itself. I have the greatest life as a performer, and being able to share that with people is nothing short of magical. My fans are the ones who inspire me to continue to create new music for them. It is their encouragement and passion that drive me to get creative and come up with new material, get back on the road and perform for them at shows around the world."

Screenwriter Katherine T. Koonce talks about what gave her the creative desire to write the screenplay *The Ladder House View*. Katherine is a former winner of the African American Women in Cinema Screenplay Contest and semi-finalist in the WriteMovies screenplay contest. "I was touched by a true story of a close relative's very difficult childhood and I wanted to share my story with others. I considered writing a novel at first, but I discovered that I sensed it more visually as a script and thus wrote as such."

Inspiration begins with a thought and may lead you to create something never before seen or done.

Theatrical producer, writer, and performer Frannie Sheridan speaks of entertainment and inspiration and why the message is so important in her live theatrical works. Frannie is the sole writer and performer of her solo live show, *Confessions of a Jewish Shiksa . . . Dancing on Hitler's Grave*, which took five years to complete and which is character driven and funny yet dark. Frannie is also the host of her comedy show, *I Tried to Be Normal but It Was Taken*, celebrating diversity and multiculturalism, and *The Waltonsteins,* an original dramatic play based on her family story. "Whatever joy or message audience members derive from seeing my show is marvelous. My prayer is that it will not only entertain but inspire."

If your work entertains and inspires, you are an artist.

FOLLOW YOUR BELIEFS

Follow your beliefs. If you feel you can create, do it.

Author Steve Alten, who penned the *New York Times* bestseller

Meg, talks about writing, belief, and inspiration, and states that his ideas for books come from articles, books, dreams, television, and just daydreaming. "I always believed I could write, but what transformed belief into action was a 1995 *Time* magazine article I read on the Mariana Trench. That spurred an idea of a giant shark I had read about when I was a teen. I set a goal that I would take thirty days and do research, then start writing every night and on weekends." Once Steve found literary manager Ken Atchity and edited that first novel, it sold in twenty-three countries worldwide. "It's been a roller-coaster ride ever since."

Belief is significant to author Madeleine Kirsh, who was inspired to create and publish her first book, *The Truth of Time,* because of the fascinating tales her clients and customers would tell her about the origins of the vintage clothing and accessories she would take on consignment at her showroom, C. Madeleine's, in Miami. "My consignors would speak about the intrinsic importance of each item and provide a glimpse of the past through their storytelling. And the stories were so amazing. I promised myself that I would one day write a book and my stories would be in the form of a diary, providing the reader with insight into the minds of the people who entered my world and who would share their legacy with me through their vintage clothing."

Promise yourself to believe in your work and make it inspirational. To be inspired and to share your art with others can be the hallmark of your artistry.

> **INSTANT REPLAY**
>
> This is about your art. Your goal as an artist is to be creative and inspired in all of your artistic endeavors. In this manner, the originality and creativity of your art should set you apart from others.

THE PATH TO ARTISTIC SUCCESS

The path to artistic success is always unique to each artist. Once you find your path, go for it!

Prelude Pictures President and CEO Daniel de Liege found that his calling in the entertainment industry was as a producer in film and television. "I was working part-time at night and going to classes during the day, but was not enjoying what I was doing. Then I met a person at a chamber of commerce event who was opening a production company that provided programming for the Discovery Channel. He told me that he thought I'd make a great television producer."

Daniel said he did not think much of it at the time, but after a few months he just picked up the phone and called his contact. It was the right call at the right time. "He offered me a job and I found myself in the entertainment business. So I learned the ropes in television and in the late 1990s I met Mark W. Koch, Chairman of Prelude Pictures, and went to work for Prelude in 1998. I worked very hard and eventually became a full partner at the company. Today I'm the head of Prelude Pictures."

Many artists find their calling in creating new content for others to see. That is a fine goal for which to strive.

DREAM AND THINK BIG

As an artist, free yourself from artificial artistic boundaries and let your creativity soar.

Commenting on why he embarked on his autobiographical screenplay, *Court of Kings*, prominent Florida Atlantic University basketball coach, speaker, author, and screenwriter Mike Jarvis stated, "If you are going to dream or think, you might as well dream and think big. I asked myself how many people would see their story on the big screen, and just the thought of it made me excited." The basketball court was the inspiration for Coach Jarvis's dream, and he envisioned a film about it. "Of course, I love reading books and also wrote one that was published. But there is something about a movie that is special."

Coach Jarvis's journey was also spiritual, and he was encouraged and inspired by his pastor, David Nicholas, during their Friday morning Bible studies. "Pastor Nicholas suggested that I had a story I needed to share, that it would be good for me personally to share it, and that it could also help and motivate other people. And the more I thought about it, the more I felt it should be told. You see, everyone's got a story, but everyone is not necessarily in a position to share that story with others. I was, and wanted to."

Stories are what the world is made of, and creative stories drive the entertainment industry.

Screenwriter Robin Abramovitz Goldberg, in commenting on her decision to write a screenplay for a film project, stated, "I was inspired by my years as a young professional in New York City and wrote about it, titling my work *Bing's Place*. In my mind, I wanted the characters to come alive just as in real life, and I created a screenplay for it. That is not to say a good book can't do the same, but I visualized it as a film."

So let your artistic and creative voice be heard, whether it is by the pen, the voice, on screen, or on stage.

YOUR ARTISTIC SKILLS

Your creativity as an artist will define you as an individual and a talent.

The late author Mark Poncy brought his considerable writing skills to the forefront with his fascinating book, *Revelation.* "It has always seemed to me that there are tradeoffs one makes when writing a novel or a screenplay. The former is long on thought, the second action-rooted. The challenge is to make the novel compelling enough to sweep the reader into just having to turn the page, largely as a substitute for action."

Mark felt that the challenge of the screenplay was to add enough introspection to give the characters the kind of depth that attracts us to the novel format. His choice was the book, and he wanted to engage the reader in his story, forcing imaginative thought as the plot unraveled in order to bring a compelling concept to the world where science meets science fiction.

Author and Jules Verne scholar George Rios was inspired to translate a Jules Verne classic into the English language. His adaptation, *Masters of the Sea: The Adventures of Jules Verne's Mathias Sandorf*, was the result of that inspiration.

George states that as a youngster, he was fascinated with literature, music, and languages, studying Latin, French, and Spanish in school. "My interest in classical music also required language skill development. When I served in the U.S. Army in France, I began to read French literature and rediscovered the science fiction of Jules Verne in the original French text. I loved the story and my goal was to translate it."

It should be your goal to challenge and create in your art. Life is expressed within your art and, conversely, art is expressed within your life.

THE EXPRESSION AND SPIRIT OF LIFE IN ART

As an artist, you must always express yourself.

Prominent ActTrue director and acting coach Marc Durso remarks, "We study life, and life is timeless. Technologies and styles may change, but that which connects us all is the human struggle for life. It is there that we must begin our artistic journey so that our work is based on the truth of humanity, not the façade of 'the biz.'"

Marc feels that the study of life permits us to understand how fascinating our artistic world can be and how it may give us direction. We can then chart our course toward personal and artistic success.

The visual arts reflect the artist's insight into expressions of life in art.

Maxim Kantor is regarded as one of the finest living abstract visual artists. Born in Moscow, his works have been exhibited throughout Western Europe and the United States.

Maxim's inspiration began at an early age. When asked when he first decided he would like to be a visual artist and sculptor, he replied, "When I was four, I began to draw. There is a photo in which

I am depicted drawing a battle of knights. When I was six, I started to write novels. The first one was about pirates. And when I was ten, my father bought me oil to paint." Maxim knew his path existed in the visual arts. "I wanted to be an artist and a writer from the very beginning. There was a short period, when I was eight or nine, that I had a strong wish to be Robin Hood, but I think that in a way I fulfilled this desire too, living vicariously through my works."

Maxim envisions a concept in his mind before creating a painting, etching, or sculpture. "It is all very strange. You can think for days, months, and years about your future picture. You can develop a concept, but when you take a brush you have to be spontaneous. Of course, I do have definite plans on how to do that and in principle I have a clear vision for my future work. But since artwork is a passion, it always brings surprises."

Artists exude a strong spirit, which is important for creativity. The expression of life in art does not exist alone. It is an integral part of creativity.

WHEN INSPIRATION FOSTERS IMAGINATION: THE WRITER

Inspiration, writing, and imagination are partners to the artist.

Maryann Ridini Spencer is the President of Ridini Entertainment Corporation in Los Angeles and is a writer, producer, host, and journalist. Maryann speaks about what inspires her imagination and creativity. "My inspiration lives in life relationships (friends and family) and reading everything; magazines, newspapers, blogs, novels, and nonfiction. I'm also inspired by seeing a variety of movies in all genres, viewing paintings and photography, and listening to music. I allow myself time to think while I'm on a walk in nature outside of my home in California, or driving to a vacation destination. Daily writing is also important to keep the ideas flowing, whether I'm working on a story concept, putting together a newsletter, or writing a blog article."

Alexandria Xiaoli Zheng, author of the novel *Forbidden Symphony*, also comments on the need for a writer to embrace inspiration and imagination. "Besides the language skills, a writer must tell a story that inspires others. To create an inspirational story, you need to be a philosopher, and that requires daily experience as well as willingness, learning, thinking, and passion."

And authors Lazaro (Laz) Mur and Arlen Castillo felt the same way when they undertook the fascinating task of creating and writing an original cookbook, *Now You're Cooking with Latin Flavors*, which provides interesting and novel recipes from Cuba and Nicaragua, their respective countries of origin. Arlen states, "We thought it would be original for us to share our heritage in our own words."

Think about your goals as an artist and have an artistic and imaginative mindset. Be inspired and creative in all that you do, while you choose to share your art with others and the world.

INSTANT REPLAY

Your inspiration should be reflected in your art; that will define your path to success. As an artist, you should always approach your work based upon original and dynamic thought.

Challenge yourself creatively and always remember that life is expressed in art. Be inspired, creative, and imaginative.

GREAT ART REQUIRES GREAT TIMING

Great art is always intertwined with great timing.

Television personality and super-chef Ingrid Hoffman loves her career and finds it very satisfying, stating that it has translated into success. She explains, "I stayed focused and worked '24/7,' which I still do. It has required great sacrifice on a personal, family level, but that's what it takes."

Ingrid feels that the creation of great art requires very fine timing. "Satisfaction and success are a combination of things. In my case, the timing was right for modern Latin food and a Latin chef, since this was not offered on television, and my concept of easy everyday food with a Latin twist was relatable not only for that market, but also for the Anglo market."

Ingrid also believes that she built a great strategy based upon the extensive research she had done, choosing to stay the course and work hard for very little money just to be able to build her media presence.

Timing is everything in art. If you plan to create great art, understand the importance of timing and give it all that you have to give.

YOUR ARTISTIC ROOTS

Your artistic roots make you who you are. Always respect them as you move forward in the creation of your work.

Real Housewives of Miami television personality and art gallery dealer Adriana De Moura speaks about the visual arts and its unique nature within the arts, stating that personal satisfaction must come from within. "First, be original," she states. "Make your art something that has not been done before. That is particularly important since it is a main criterion for success when it comes to merchandizing your works. Second, be prolific. You must have enough of your work out there so that it will be available for many people to see. Third, try to secure good representation with a gallery that loves your work and has great contacts. If the gallery accepts your work for financial reasons alone, then it may be difficult to move those pieces."

Though their artistic works may be unique, all artists share traits that begin early in life and define each artist as an individual.

Jenna Edwards, a former Ms. Florida USA and president of the For a Day Foundation, found her artistic roots in her art early on, beginning with the pageant process as a child in Mississippi.

She simply loved what she was doing. "Being from a small town in Mississippi, many people saw pageants as a way to 'see the world.' Beauty queens were revered in the community and little girls lined up for autographs. My dance teacher ran the local Miss Clinton pageant and she marketed the crown to our class. When my mother picked me up from class, I declared 'I want that crown,' and the rest is history." Jenna dug in and continued to develop her art, finding her work to be personally satisfying.

Personal satisfaction, when linked with creativity within the arts, has many different meanings to different people. To be creative as an artist, regardless of the genre, is to be willing to rely upon your artistic roots and the outer realm of your imagination in order to develop and define new and innovative thought, and to help shape new ideas and concepts in your artistic way.

INSTANT REPLAY

Great art requires artistic timing. And timing in the creation of your art can define the nature and style of your craft. Let your artistic roots lead you to new creative horizons.

THE ORIGINALITY OF AN ARTISTIC CONCEPT

What is it that makes your artistic concept original?

Diana Lozano talks about originality in the world of modern dance. "By denotation, 'original' simply means that it was done first. However, I don't believe that something that is done first makes it more or less valuable. For me, it's about the work and thought process behind a concept or piece. We live in a re-mix culture, and all artists are inspired and influenced by the myriad of artists before them."

Carolina Garcia-Aguilera also remarks about originality. "My books are very visual. I am a storyteller who has a story to tell. "When my children were growing up, I would tell them stories that included a character, and each night I made up a new chapter. So when my kids were very young, I would tell them about a fish from Brazil named 'Ish-Fish,' who would visit different oceans by jumping on the top of an airplane and flying to the next ocean, where he would jump off. And that is how they learned about the different countries of the world."

As an artist, find the originality of your work as your art begins to define itself.

A PASSION FOR YOUR WORK

Your work must reflect your passion as an artist, regardless of your genre.

Fine art and commercial photographer Lynn Parks has traveled throughout the United States, Europe, and South America to photograph her subjects. Lynn was asked what brought her to the artistic world of photography and the creation of her original works.

"It was my passion for art and fashion. Capturing subjects digitally and on film has been an amazing and fantastic journey. I've been a photographer for over 23 years, and it has been a pleasure to make a living as a photographic artist. I try to make my images capture intimate and private moments, and I look for both realism and sensuality in my photographs. When I shoot 'the' shot, I just know it is right. I can feel the excitement of an exquisite photograph and it gives me great satisfaction in my work."

Vocalist and songwriter David Brigati, a former Decca and Roulette Records recording artist who has performed with Joey Dee and the Starliters and the Young Rascals, speaks about his artistic voice and a passion for music. "My inspiration was in performing the song and hearing my voice on the radio. Regarding any song you sing, your initial impulse is to test yourself against what you hear over the air. Inspiration translates into a sense of enjoyment, which translates back again into inspiration."

It is the artist's passion for his or her art that defines the quality of the work. And it is the passion of the work that marks the quality of the artist.

ART THAT SPEAKS TO OTHERS

Art is a universal language that speaks to others around the world.

Robin Abramovitz Goldberg commented on that language and the message it brings as she wrote her screenplay. "I wanted to write a story that would make a change in people's lives. I wanted people to understand that they have second chances, that they are not alone, and that everyone carries a story inside."

Being original in your work can be critical to your reputation as an artist. To create new boundaries in your craft permits you to speak to others through your art as you establish yourself within the industry.

YOUR CREATIVITY FROM WITHIN

Creativity lives within the artist.

Though the artist's vision, imagination, and direction define his or her work, the work can also define the artist, presenting a very individualized and stylized picture of the creative force that lies within. It makes no difference whether artists are emerging within their respective fields, have "arrived" and are beginning to taste success, or are already successful role models for others but wish to continue to explore their art in new and challenging directions.

So why do we do what we do in this industry? And why is it not just a position or profession, but a state of mind and a calling?

That is because artistic individuals must express themselves through their artistry. It is the focus within and through their creative expression that will bring artistic recognition and success. In essence, the industry cannot exist without the creative force of the artist. And it is artists who make the industry what it is.

Diana Lozano believes that if one is interpreting art like a product, then like with any product, it will be adapted and refined through the generations. She feels that art can simply be a mirror held up to society. "If you are interpreting art in its purest sense, then whether or not something is technically original is a non-issue. What makes it original is your interpretation of it. What matters is whether the work accomplishes a purpose, whatever that may be, whether it is to connect, enlighten, or provoke humanity."

Your creativity from within can be the basis of all great art that you may develop. Your art will reflect your determination as an artist.

ARTISTIC DISCOVERY

Artistic discovery is at the center of creativity and exists in all fields of the arts.

It lives in the world of music.

When asked why he performs, New York classical pianist and composer James Adler commented, "As a performer, I want to share the joy of discovery with my audience when I step onto a concert stage. I try to communicate the composer's intentions, stylistically and with emotion. As a composer, I try to express passion and intellect through my music while communicating with audiences."

It also lives in the written word.

Ken Atchity comments on why he initially entered the world of literary management. "When I left the academic world to produce movies, I realized that managing stories and storytellers was my strength. When I discovered literary management, I had found the 'promised land,' and my mission was to bring talented writers across the river to their professional destiny."

Artistic discovery exists in all artistic genres throughout the world and is the creative foundation for great art.

PURSUING YOUR DREAMS

An artist who is committed to his or her work will always pursue the dream of creating art.

Robin Abramovitz Goldberg comments, "Never give up! If you have a story that you want to share, pick up a piece of paper or open your computer and take notes. Carry those notes with you, and always be ready to write down new thoughts or observations, since you never know where or when an inspiring idea may come your way. Just write it down when it does. Even a cocktail napkin and a pen will do for that next great novel, screenplay, poem, or song."

Gabe Berman, a freelance writer for the *Miami Herald* and author of the book *Live Like a Fruit Fly,* suggests, "Pick up a pen or flip open your laptop tonight. Don't wait any longer. The world is rotating with or without you. You can't be a writer unless you're writing."

Pursue your artistic dreams. Art is the result of such commitment.

THE RESILIENCE OF THE HUMAN SPIRIT IN ART

The world can be a turbulent place to live. Yet the artistic spirit survives.

Dr. James (Jamie) Huysman, PsyD, LCSW, CAP, CFT, is an authority, speaker, and media expert on advising those within the industry who suffer from caregiver burnout, compassion fatigue, and addictions. He speaks about the resilience of the human spirit in art and the commitment of the artist to his or her art.

When Jamie appeared on network television, he had a platform upon which to reach people. Speaking to large audiences through the media was his artistic gift, and he used it to the best of his abilities. "Be prepared to sacrifice everything and forget about money or becoming a top celebrity. The intention is to be in sync with your inner self and realize the sacrifice and joy in the process."

Artists live for art that is resilient and that defines their own works.

YOUR ARTISTIC PERSEVERANCE

It is the very nature of the creative arts that inspires creativity and perseverance from within.

You are the captain and navigator of your own artistic ship and can control and direct your artistic destiny, making creative decisions that will have a lasting effect on the opportunities ahead and the chances for success. And as you move onward toward your stated goals in life, your art will evolve, just as you do as an individual. Thus, you should remain positive and passionate about your art.

Remembering that art is a creative force in and of itself, you must realize that the art that is created will be initially defined by you, its creator. It is that artistic definition that will become the starting point for understanding, evaluating, and critiquing your work going forward.

INSTANT REPLAY

Always persevere in the creation of your original art. Explore your work and discover new artistic boundaries, never giving up your quest to create great work. Let your spirit soar in the creation of your art.

STORIES WITHIN YOUR ART AND THE MESSAGE THAT ART GIVES US

All great art tells a story.

This is true whether we speak of the lyrics to a song, any particular style of music, ballet or modern dance, the plot of a suspenseful screenplay or novel, a teleplay or screenplay on television or the big screen, a work of the visual arts such as a painting or photograph, or any other aspect of the arts.

In the end, it is the story that makes the piece original and compelling. As the artist, it's all about your story. And only you can tell it the way it was meant to be told.

THE HERO'S JOURNEY IN LITERARY MYTHOLOGY

How do stories evolve within the arts and where do they originate?

Perhaps the most significant theory postulated about the art of the story was presented in the concept known as "The Hero's Journey," made famous by the late author Joseph Campbell. Many consider this writing model to be the centerpiece of creative storytelling in all the arts. Campbell's book, *The Hero with a Thousand Faces,* was first published in 1949 and is considered the author's definitive work on the topic of comparative mythology and the essence of storytelling.

In that book, Campbell presents us with his theory of the journey of the hero prevalent in world mythology. He explains the existence of a basic and fundamental structure to myths from around the world, which he calls the "monomyth." In the monomyth, the hero ventures forth from the everyday world into a place of great wonder, which Campbell labels "the call to adventure." It is there that the hero encounters incredible obstacles and challenges, identified as "a road of trials."

Yet through our hero's valiant efforts, the destination is reached and important self-knowledge is discovered. Armed with that self-knowledge, a decision is made to return to the everyday world. Still, our hero encounters new obstacles and challenges on the return trip and surmounts them, successfully arriving back to the everyday world and sharing this new knowledge with all humankind.

Like our hero in "The Hero's Journey," the creative artist makes an artist's journey, traveling to a different realm in order to find the truth in his or her art. And our artist may be confronted with many barriers to artistic success along this path, some of which may seem at times to be insurmountable. Yet the artist moves forward because of the desire to find artistic truth and the need to continue to create new art and introduce it to the world. In the end, our artist returns safely home to bring his or her art to others, providing new and fascinating insights into art heretofore not seen. That is the artist's journey.

Great art presents a message, and the more poignant and significant the message is, the more important it is that it be delivered. So follow your artist's journey in creating your art so that others may appreciate and enjoy it.

INSTANT REPLAY

The mythology of storytelling is unique to your art and reflects your message to the world, establishing you as an individual and an artist.

AND IT'S A WRAP

And it's a wrap, with some thoughts for your consideration.

You should aspire to create great art, and you have the artistic right to let your work reflect your world as you envision it. Think as a free spirit and be original, inspired, and imaginative when creating your work. The industry will welcome it.

Do not compromise your art. Be artistically honest with yourself and be true to your work as you share it with the world for everyone to see, appreciate, and enjoy.

FILM

- ★ The motion picture industry consists of many moving parts, and you are one of them. It takes a lot to make a movie, and in film, creativity and originality must be considered in conjunction with artistic and commercial appeal in order to find an audience.

- ★ Be focused on developing your reputation in the industry and set your short- and long-term goals. Above all, be creative and original in your thinking and your work. Hollywood loves talent, and to be there and find success demonstrates to the world that you have what it takes.

- ★ Remember that films take time to make and artistic visions can change or morph into new concepts or visions that are entirely different from those initially presented. Follow your creative dreams in film. The rewards will be worth the effort.

TELEVISION

- ★ Television provides a medium of creative expression in which content is generally developed and created in a shorter period of time than film. However, the same rules apply with regard to the presentation of that content, which must be professionally crafted to be considered.

★ The television industry rewards those who are gifted, such as producers, directors, writers, and actors. Without question, artistry lives in the world of television. Look for opportunities there. They can move at the speed of light, and you do not want to miss them.

MUSIC

★ The music industry is undergoing incredibly rapid changes in its structure because of the digitization of the industry and the transformation of the distribution mechanism.

★ Today, there are more opportunities than ever before for a recording artist to find an audience. And in the end, original and creative music is still critical to artistic and commercial success.

THE LITERARY ARTS

★ The publishing industry, like the music industry, is also in the midst of significant changes because of the explosive growth of ebooks and the rise of the independent or vanity publishing companies.

★ Still, great authors with superb stories will always find their way through this maze of changes and onto the shelves of bookstores.

FASHION AND MODELING

★ More so than in many other fields, fashion and modeling represent a culture that is constantly changing, both in direction and texture.

★ Here, creativity becomes a moving object in a universe of style. The moment you touch it, it changes again. In this business, you must move fast in order to stay at the forefront.

THE VISUAL ARTS AND THE FINE ARTS

★ The visual arts and the fine arts will always be with us, as long as there is a canvas upon which to paint or sketch, a camera to capture an image, or a stage upon which to perform.

Originality and creativity thrive in this environment and often cut through the outer edge of the envelope in art.

LIGHTS, CAMERA, ACTION!

You are unique as an artist and you have something very special to give to the world. However, to understand the true nature of the entertainment industry, you must begin to understand its business.

And business is what the commercial side of the industry is all about, which will be discussed in the next chapter.

A STORY INSPIRED BY A LITERARY MANAGER AND WRITING COACH

It began as just five short, concise sentences that presented the concept for a story, and nothing more.

As a prominent literary manager and writing coach, he found the idea to be interesting and envisioned it as an independent film.

So he advised his client, an emerging screenwriter, to simply express her thoughts in the form of a treatment and eventually create a screenplay.

And the process began. Under his direction, she started to write.

It had taken her what seemed like forever, beginning with the logline and treatment. Once he reviewed both and made suggestions, which she incorporated into her work, she began to draft the screenplay.

The writer was excited about the project and somewhat anxious to have it completed while she carefully followed his instructions to ensure that the story would be original, dynamic, and compelling.

She would often ask him when it would be done. The answer he would provide was that they would both know the screenplay was done when it was done, and not a moment before. He made it clear that this would not be based upon some predetermined formula, but upon solid creative writing. In essence, that decision would be made when the last word was written and the final revision was complete.

That day would certainly come, but it was not here yet.

And so the writing process would continue. She went through so many edited versions that she lost count.

As she wrote, the story continued to develop and the characters became animated. The traits and quirks of each character were illuminated until they were almost larger than life. And the script reflected drama and conflict, the essential ingredients of a great story.

Under the manager's wise and patient counsel, she continued her work until the characters seemed to literally jump off the pages of the screenplay, filling the reader with excitement.

In time, she completed a full first draft of the script and sent it to him, asking what he thought of her writing. She waited to hear back from him.

Then his email came, asking her for a conference.

Holding her breath, she called him at the appointed time.

As she listened, he spoke about the story and paused for a moment. To her, it seemed like an eternity. Then he told her the screenplay was good. In fact, it was very good. Now it was time for him to polish it and after that, he would speak to her about the next steps, including his plans to contact an agent and producer on her behalf.

The writer was overjoyed and breathed a sigh of relief. She asked him what else she could do in the interim.

He simply said, "Begin working on your next screenplay. That's what writers do. And you're a writer."

And that is what she did.

He is a renowned literary manager, writing coach, film and television producer, and CEO of Atchity Entertainment International, Inc. He is also a teacher, writer, poet, and lyricist.

He is Dr. Kenneth J. Atchity.

And he is an artist.

TWO

THE BUSINESS OF THE ENTERTAINMENT INDUSTRY

Step into my plastic home, I'll promise you a thrill
Deep inside where dreams can't hide away
Have a seat, and sip some tea,
I'm sure we'll pass the time
There's nothing like an evening with the radio.

Richard Warren Rappaport,
"There's Nothing Like an Evening with the Radio,"
from the motion picture soundtrack of *Concert*

THE BASICS

This chapter is about the business of the entertainment industry. It addresses entertainment as a business and the importance of enhancing your opportunities for the attainment of success in your art. Insights into the workings of the commercial world and the delicate balance that exists between your artistry and commercialism are discussed, as well as the creativity, inspiration, beauty, and quality of your art in such a setting.

The entertainment industry has become what some call a "spinning paradigm," and the rapid changes within that industry are analyzed along with their effects on today's media and the world of distribution of artistic content.

Your role in today's business environment is discussed as well as the need to remain true to your dreams and the opportunities that may arise. The balance between money and artistry and the commercial value of your art is considered, and the challenges faced by the "indie" or independent artist are explored. As an example, the filmmaker's dilemma in the search for success is described.

Lastly, new approaches to distribution and guerilla marketing are reviewed with an eye toward how you may create your own strategy tailored to your needs as an artist.

WHY THIS CHAPTER IS IMPORTANT TO YOU

If the artistry of the entertainment industry is based on its creativity, the business of the entertainment industry brings that creativity to the world.

FILM

* The film industry is based upon a series of solid business models that underlie its entire artistic and corporate structure. To find success in the industry, you should have a clear understanding of the nature of that business.

* Look carefully for the ground rules and follow industry protocol. Above all, respect the system for what it is. If you are good, you will rise to the top.

TELEVISION

★ As with film, television relies very heavily on its business structure and the strategic positions of the players who make up the networks that air practically all that is seen on television today. As with film, structure and protocol are paramount.

★ Creativity and business make a powerful partnership in television. This can carry you to the realization of your goals.

MUSIC

★ The music industry is in the midst of being digitally reborn, and the individuals today who are setting new goals in the creation and distribution of music are tomorrow's pioneers.

★ If any industry is subject to practically instantaneous change, it is this industry. As with film and television, understand the business structure, but expect it to change at the blink of an eye.

THE LITERARY ARTS

★ While the music industry is morphing rapidly, the publishing industry is not far behind. The old models of distribution are crumbling and the new models may only be temporary, to be followed by newer ones.

★ As with music, the Internet is redefining the business structure. Be aware of this and look to the future. That is where you will find great books and great authors.

FASHION AND MODELING

★ Business propels fashion and modeling domestically and internationally. The world lives on fashion and loves being in fashion. And modeling goes hand in hand with fashion.

★ Fashion and modeling are constantly redefining themselves and setting the new business trends for tomorrow's runways. Just as you follow fashion, follow the business trends that power it.

THE VISUAL ARTS AND THE FINE ARTS

★ Visual artists who work on canvas or in photography know that business is what brings their artistic works to the world.

★ The fine arts are just as much about business as all other aspects of the arts.

— THE COURT OF ARTISTIC OPINION —
"COUNSELORS, APPROACH THE BENCH"

Once again, you slowly open the hallway doors and peek through into the Court of Artistic Opinion.

The court is not yet in session, but the room is no longer dark and empty. There are spectators in the courtroom waiting for everyone to arrive. Your artistry has not yet been presented to the world. When it is, court will be in session. And that will happen sooner than you think.

By understanding the business of the entertainment industry, you will significantly enhance your chances for success. The next stop is the world of business in the entertainment industry.

ENTERTAINMENT AS A BUSINESS AND THE BUSINESS OF ENTERTAINMENT

In order to find success within the industry, you must make artistic and business decisions that may have a profound effect upon your career. In Chapter One, the artistry of your work was discussed.

Now the focus has shifted to that realm where the worlds of creativity, artistry, and business meet and sometimes collide. In this context, always remember that your goal as an artist must remain clear. Be true to your art and, if you wish, present it to the world to enjoy and appreciate.

OPPORTUNITIES FOR THE ATTAINMENT OF SUCCESS

If your goal is, in part, the attainment of success within the entertainment industry, you must realize that it requires a complete and unwavering commitment to that goal. However, to achieve success, you must have a working understanding of the commercial nature of the industry as well as the opportunities present within the new industry paradigm that exists today. You must also understand the new industry paradigm's impact on marketing and distribution, especially in the marketplace for independent projects.

It is also important to be aware of that very delicate and subtle balance between commercialism and true artistry. Once that balance is understood, it will enhance the likelihood of finding success so that the artistry within your work and the commercial nature of the industry can find a dynamic medium.

Most important, in order for you to have the greatest opportunity to find critical and financial success, you must have a team. And that team, discussed in Chapter Three, will define the level and degree of success by providing the essential expertise in law and business that is needed at critical times during the course of this artistic and commercial journey.

INSTANT REPLAY

As the artist, you must understand the business of entertainment. In this manner, you will enhance your opportunities for the attainment of success for your art in the commercial world.

COMMERCIALISM IN THE ENTERTAINMENT INDUSTRY

The business of the entertainment industry is to provide entertainment with commercial appeal, depending on the demographic segment of the market that is the focus of the art. It is also important that the artist's work is financially viable, which requires that his or her art be properly introduced to the industry.

As previously stated, your goal as an artist should be to create great art and strive for excellence within your field. This is particularly relevant because ultimately you must understand that the creative process should always exist during the course of your career. That is the very nature of your creative work.

THE BALANCE BETWEEN ARTISTRY AND COMMERCIALISM

Commercialism has a very different meaning to each artist. That meaning may define the direction and eventual artistic and financial success of the artist.

When asked how she advises artists on finding the true balance between the artistry of what they do and the commercial nature of the entertainment industry, producer Maryann Ridini Spencer simply states, "Artistry and business go hand in hand. While managers, agents, and attorneys are there to assist the artist, that artist needs to be aware of every aspect of his or her career and be kept up to speed on how the industry operates."

And associate classical music producer Regina Rachael comments, "In essence, you need both ears; one for the music itself and the other for the commercial market for which it is intended."

The balance between artistry and commercialism may seem to be extremely delicate and difficult to define. Yet many times the artist instinctively knows where that balance lies, and that can result in the launch of a career.

CREATIVITY, INSPIRATION, AND THE COMMERCIAL WORLD

Creativity and inspiration in art and the commercial world can and often do find common ground.

Producer and literary manager Ken Atchity discusses creativity, inspiration, and commercialism in the literary arts, explaining, "Success in the publishing world has three distinct but critical and integral elements: a high-concept story that is original, the ability to execute the story in writing or to have another writer accomplish that for you, and access to a seller who will have access to buyers in the market."

Bob Berkowitz, president of Multivision Video and Film, produces in film, television, and multimedia. "So often a creative idea, screenplay, or show outline comes across my desk and I know there is no hope of it ever seeing the light of day. We have developed a litmus test for the viability of projects that must take precedence over emotional response and creative pride. In essence, we ask ourselves, 'Can this thing sell? If it's produced, will anyone want to see it, sponsor it, or better yet, pay for it?' These are questions the creator often finds quite elusive as the realities of the budget, market, and media come into play."

What you may learn is that if you wish to find commercial success, it is not enough that you create great art that has meaning and significance. You must also grasp and accept the business and artistic parameters of the commercial market for that art in order to attain your goals and find artistic and financial success. Of course, when a great artist finds a great producer, magic can happen. Both are talented, and great talent always finds its way.

INSTANT REPLAY

As an artist, you must learn how to be realistic and deal with the commercial world. Once you achieve that, the balance you reach between artistry and commercialism will define your work and the likelihood for commercial success.

THE NEW INDUSTRY PARADIGM

What is this new industry paradigm in the world of entertainment?

In essence, the new paradigm reflects the rapid evolution of the business and market dynamics of the industry, being driven by major technological changes in the creation, duplication, and distribution of artistic content in all its forms. These changes are so dynamic that you, the artist, must make it your business to be informed and up to date on how the new age will impact the presentation of your art.

This will require a very comprehensive understanding of the creative process and its artistic and commercial applications, as well as protocol within the industry and the new nature of distribution.

AN EXAMPLE IN LITERARY MANAGEMENT

Ken Atchity regards the industry as not only a moving paradigm, but one that is spinning, to the extent that it seems at times practically impossible to keep up with the technology and consumer reaction to it. Ken claims that in the film and book publishing industries, these myriad changes caused him to create some critical shifts in his company's business and marketing plans.

Specifically, the new paradigm has had a profound effect on standard literary management.

Ken states, "Aside from a handful of clients who are making good money, changes have taken our company, AEI, out of standard literary management, where you put in present effort for far-future dollars, and into career coaching, meaning a present effort for present dollars." Interestingly, Ken sees a silver lining in his newest line of work. "I have found that in this new coaching business, StoryMerchant.com, I actually get to spend unpressured time with my clients instead of being forced to focus on just the ones who are earning money right now. That's what I've always loved the most about advising writers."

To underscore the importance of an awareness of the changes,

Ken voices his opinion on the film industry and the effect of this new paradigm on it. "Although people are watching movies more than ever before based on industry statistics, the major studios have cut back their movie making to 10 percent or 15 percent of what it was a few short years ago. Unless you're already a household name, getting them to look at your novel or spec script almost requires miracles, not that we haven't done a few of those."

And to make matters more difficult, the paradigm is still constantly morphing. Ken suggests, "The independent film market is in a perennial renaissance. Movies are being made and Oscars are being awarded. The problem here is that there's virtually no development money for optioning properties or turning novels into screenplays." Ken provides a caveat to his clients who are writers. "If you want to break in, and you're my client or partner, I'm going to coach you to become a proactive filmmaker."

And as for the world of television, he comments, "The television movie is all but dead these days, though I believe it will return. Reality and dramatic series are where it's at, but both have specific appetites and both are difficult to break into. At my companies, we're fortunate that we've shot two reality shows recently, and are in preproduction with two movies, and casting for another."

In fact, the changes are practically exponential, causing those who wish to find success engaged in a constant struggle to maintain their course. On dealing with this type of business environment, Ken says, "We keep an open mind, and an eye on rapidly changing events to allow us to protect our clients' interests."

To simply maintain your artistic pace is not enough in these times. In this new paradigm, you must be either on top of or ahead of the business curve in order to have a clear vision of your direction.

ART AS A MOVING TARGET IN TODAY'S MEDIA

Today, art in the commercial world never stops changing as tastes and interests change.

Television personality Ingrid Hoffman states, "Everything in today's media environment is a moving target and so you also have to be moving. You should try to stay ahead of the rest."

Personal and business manager Wayne B. Baxley agrees. Wayne manages the nationally known comedienne Sommore, who is also his wife. "The entertainment industry is morphing by the way it is viewed and perceived by others. Today, most people don't see 'stand-up' as a serious profession that is difficult to attain in the same way they may see singers, athletes, or actors attaining success. That is because they see so much comic content out there, whether on television or the Internet, that they assume that anyone can do it. Actually, the art of stand-up is a very unique profession, and although it may appear to be easy to do, it is very far from that and requires a great deal of time and study in order for a good comedian or comedienne to perfect the craft."

Many within the industry, including Ken Atchity, feel that the marketplace is ultimately the great equalizer. In this respect, Ken suggests, "Amid the turmoil of the changing channels of delivery, one thing remains constant in the story marketplace: the worldwide demand for great stories and important information, which makes creating and owning intellectual property an even more stable opportunity."

This dynamic shift within the entire industry is creating changes at a very rapid rate, making it all the more important to maintain your pace and keep up with such changes in order to stay on top of your artistic game. But you must if you wish to attain commercial success.

THE MORPHING OF THE INDUSTRY

What are other industry insiders saying about the morphing of the entertainment industry?

Los Angeles entertainment attorney Peter Dekom has very clear opinions on how the industry is morphing and how that may affect its future. "The paradigm shift from analog to digital has turned the industry upside down. Film library value is eroding because no one can really grant 'exclusive' rights in a digital world."

Peter feels the significance of this cannot be overstated. "Regardless of how you feel about piracy, content becomes pretty ubiquitous in a digital world. And where money is paid, it is often trading away the dollars per consumer we used to make for the pennies that are the result of cheap streaming or downloading sites now substituted for home video and pay television."

Has the system eroded to the extent that profitable projects may soon cease to exist? It is at least an issue that is on the table throughout the industry, as executives try to find a way to create new models of distribution.

DISTRIBUTION IN THE NEW PARADIGM

What about the effects on distribution in the new paradigm?

Peter states, "Consumers are telling studios when, how, and where they want their movies distributed, and studios that resist have the highest piracy numbers. This has effectively pushed the revenue efforts forward and into the earliest time period in the distribution pipeline. Gone is the value of the 'long tail' in distribution and in its place is a move to gather all the money as fast as possible while the getting is still good."

Peter tells us that the impact of this is evidenced in the constant moving of the release dates of content in the digital aftermarket. "Inevitably, the rule will be the day and release date of theatrical films in theaters and across multiple platforms. Aftermarkets, contrary to filmmaker expectations, will continue to erode in value."

Back in the world of book publishing, our spinning paradigm is about to spin out of control. Ken Atchity suggests, "Publishing is now focused on 'fear' and 'brands.' Fear is a focus because although downloads of the ebook are around 15 percent and are still a minor percentage of the market, no one wants to be the last operating publisher in the real-book business, holding the buggy whip while everyone else is driving an iPad or Kindle."

Ken claims that brands are also a focus because they are great insurance against the unknown in the marketplace. "Last year we 'branded' a book with a major historical name and sold it for nearly $2 million dollars worldwide, a book that would otherwise probably not have sold at all."

So while the experts ponder the commercial future of art within the industry, you must constantly evaluate the quality of your artistic work and understand your role, not only in the presentation of that work, but in the ways the work should be marketed.

> **INSTANT REPLAY**
>
> Your art must continue to be original and unique. Be aware of the signifi-
> cant and dramatic changes that are occurring in the industry, because
> understanding this new paradigm will be crucial to your success.

THE ARTIST'S ROLE WITHIN THE NEW INDUSTRY PARADIGM

What is your role within this new paradigm? How do you maintain
intellectual and artistic honesty and stability in the creation of your
art without compromising it in your own eyes, the eyes of your colleagues, or the eyes of the public?

If the art speaks for itself, it will be respected within the industry, regardless of the business model. And those aficionados who
appreciate the artist's work and share the vision will remain loyal.

REMAINING TRUE TO YOUR ARTISTIC DREAMS

As you follow your artistic dreams, your art reflects who you are as
a talent and artist.

Mark W. Koch, chairman of Prelude Pictures and producer of
the blockbuster film *Lost in Space,* once commented that, in today's
incredibly competitive environment, it's practically a miracle when
a motion picture is made.

Producer and actress Barbie Castro, who produced and co-starred
with Casper Van Dien and Armand Assante in the motion picture
Assumed Memories, wanted to follow her artistic dreams and create
a film that would permit her to continue to develop her skills as an
actress and learn the commercial end of the business. "My vision
was to create a quality film that would be screened in film festivals
and be available for distribution worldwide."

Miami, New Orleans, and Los Angeles entertainment attorney Emily P. Graham advises artists to remain true to their dreams in executing the vision of their artistic project in any commercial aspect of the arts, citing examples. "In music, the artist can write the song and perform it, but the song must be recorded in a great studio with a fine producer and engineer, and it is then professionally mastered for airplay to be presentable. For a film, if the artist is a director, he or she should have a solid general understanding of everything from filming angles and camera shots to scene sequences and editing, realizing that those skills are also shared by others on and off the set."

And has the new industry paradigm resulted in a "closed shop" for many artists who heretofore have found that the business is based primarily on personal and business relationships?

To some extent, perhaps this is so. The industry does seem at times to be like a door that never opens, especially for emerging artists who wish to remain true to their work but cannot find an outlet for that work in music, film, or television.

Palm Beach Gardens corporate and entertainment attorney Howard J. Wiener summarizes the issue very succinctly. "It's not what you know. It's who you know! In other words, the domino effect is based upon developing the right relationships with the right people, particularly in today's supercharged business environment."

Yet the quality of your work will shine if you are committed to excellence in your art. Your time will come when your work finds its path. For each door that closes, there will be another opportunity. At some point, a door will open and you will walk through it on your path toward success.

> **INSTANT REPLAY**
>
> Regardless of how the industry continues to develop in a commercial world, always remain true to your aspirations and understand the myriad opportunities in the new industry paradigm.

THE BALANCE BETWEEN MONEY AND ARTISTRY

From a purely commercial standpoint, an artist should be focused entirely on his or her art. Art, in and of itself, will define its own market, regardless of the size of that market. The critical point is that the art is not just good, but great.

Yet most artists and those who advise them will often be forced to consider that very delicate balance between artistry and financial gain that gives art its commercial appeal.

THE COMMERCIAL VALUE OF YOUR ART

What is the commercial value of your art?

Ken Atchity comments, "Art is primarily a form of communication, albeit of the highest order. Commerce is based on communication as well. Unless an artist reaches an audience, his or her light languishes in the darkness. The first step to balancing commerce with art is to find or define your audience and write for them, not for yourself."

In this regard, artists must understand the nature of today's commercial market. Using the music industry as an example, the music manager's job is to connect the dots on the regional level so that the artist can secure the venue for performing and drive ticket sales, including booking local television, radio, and print interviews prior to the event, so that it creates momentum for that event and future events in surrounding cities and in different parts of the country.

Remember that as an artist you are building a brand and trying to carve out that market. What is the lesson here? Do what you do best; create great art. Then fashion a personalized plan for the greatest opportunities for success in the industry.

THE CHALLENGES FACED BY THE INDEPENDENT ARTIST: AN EXAMPLE IN FILM

It seems that nowhere is the balance between artistry and money more critical than in the world of the independent artist. In thinking about emerging independent artists, the new industry paradigm presents a fascinating glimpse into today's business matrix and permits us to prognosticate about commerce of the future in the entertainment industry.

As an example, looking to the current state of the film industry, the producers of a motion picture project are ultimately responsible for the distribution and marketing of a film. The reason their positions are critically important is because without distribution and marketing, the film will not be seen by the public, either in the movie theater or on television, and its exposure on the Internet will be adversely affected.

Peter Dekom advises companies that produce films to maximize their efforts at capitalization, distribution, and marketing in order to make a project financially successful. "The assumption of so many filmmakers is that 'if we build it, they will come.' That is a false assumption. Every year, 4,000 to 5,000 feature films are shot in the English language, and these films generally find no meaningful distribution, particularly in the United States."

The secondary distribution markets are no better. Peter explains, "There is no 'direct-to-video' fallback except in certain genres, because marketing in video takes tremendous sums of money to get enough visibility to sell units." He feels that the big barrier is clearly marketing, a cost that has skyrocketed because the marketplace has segmented into so many tiny submarkets, reaching each with a different marketing structure and campaign.

The venues for screening and making money on films are obviously growing smaller, and that is a problem for all filmmakers, from the studio system to your system.

THE FILMMAKER'S DILEMMA

What is the filmmaker's dilemma and what does it mean for the artist?

Peter examines that dilemma for filmmakers today. "As the aftermarkets are eroding in a new digital universe, the emphasis is on films that can perform theatrically, films that can open easily on at least 1,200 domestic screens. This is a reverse of the trend that established itself in the heyday of pay television and home video expansion, both of which are now in serious contraction."

And Peter tells us that the equation becomes even more complicated. "Layer into this environment higher ticket prices, a lingering economic malaise, and a major reduction in the number of adults who watch films, particularly films that are primarily male driven, and you see that if you spend 5 or 10 million on producing a movie, why should a distributor add 20 to $30 million dollars in releasing costs for a film that really cannot support a wide theatrical release?"

Peter reminds us that independent filmmakers feel that their film will constitute the "1 in 1,000,000" success story, claiming that their film is the "next one." Yet he states, "Film festivals are pretty useless in building enough buzz. If a film doesn't have that buzz going into a festival, it's probably dead on arrival anyway. And creating buzz costs money. Six figures is not an unreasonable number. Yet the number of films picked up after being submitted for major festival consideration is staggeringly low. For instance, Sundance usually gets over 3,500 submissions for about 120 spots, resulting recently in fewer than 10 pick-ups, and the numbers paid on pick-ups have not been this bad in decades."

In essence, Peter feels that without massively high demand, a great budget, and high-profile talent, you will be engaged in an up-hill battle. And he feels that for the vast majority of filmmakers, if there is no meaningful distribution commitment from a legitimate distributor up front, from a financial perspective they are in all likelihood wasting their time and money in producing a vanity project that few people will ever see.

Although our example in the film industry may not necessarily be similar to other parts of the entertainment industry, it reflects the difficulty of executing a business plan in a very competitive market. And that calls for serious thought and guerilla marketing.

> ### INSTANT REPLAY
>
> The balance between money and your artistry must be examined in order for you to move forward with your career. You must also understand the challenges you will face as an independent artist in a commercial world.
>
> Though success stories may seem to be the exception and not the rule, no one has a lock on success. Make success yours.

CREATING YOUR OWN PARADIGM: INDEPENDENT DISTRIBUTION AND GUERILLA MARKETING

Guerilla marketing is the new face of domestic and international business within the entertainment industry.

YouTube, Twitter, Facebook, and others are redefining the marketing landscape, breathing new life into opportunities for independent companies as well as artists in all genres seeking to present their art to others outside the traditional channels.

Miami entertainment attorney Kimberly D. Kolback is very positive on this emerging approach for developing and developed artists, particularly in music, stating, "I love it. I think it gives a more talented artist a chance to make it in the industry when he or she may not otherwise be discovered because of a variety of reasons, not all of which have to do with talent but with relationships, such as having the right family members, knowing the right people, or having enough money or the right look, which is what seems to be required these days in order to work with any of the large entertainment companies."

In film and television, Peter Dekom speaks to this issue by posing the question as to what an indie really is, stating, "I wish I knew.

The indie market is a perilous one with virtually no demand from consumers or distributors. It's like transporting salt to the Pacific Ocean and wondering why it doesn't need it. What has changed is the ability to track consumer responses to advertising campaigns, to create campaigns that morph based on audience response, and to use trans-media efforts appropriate to each demographic and psychographic segment. Listen to the audience, for they clearly express their reactions."

Peter addresses the concept of subcampaigns, stating, "Market segmentation has created the need for lots of these subcampaigns, which in turn has driven marketing costs through the stratosphere. This is a really bad omen for indies, who are capital impaired in making a film and almost capital barren when it comes to marketing films. Even virtual prints require the distributor to pay the exhibitor a virtual print fee to amortize the cost of those expensive new digital projectors."

It does seem to be tough for indies in these times. Yet they survive and break through. In the end, it really does seem to be all about the quality of content.

THE IMPORTANCE OF GREAT CONTENT

How important is great content for the artist?

Peter feels that even the prospect of great marketing in the industry will not save content that is not professionally crafted or well done. "If the film is no good, then on the day it opens, the numbers will slide down fast as the audience registers their reactions by twittering and texting their comments like the ripples from a large rock hurled into a stagnant pool. You can't hide a bad movie anymore."

And Peter tells us the tolerance for failure in the film industry today is almost nonexistent. "What the studios did by forcing an increase in ticket prices was to push the threshold for 'go to a theater and see a move' much farther out. Consumers have to feel the movie is 'worthy' of the extra bucks, so if it is under-marketed, theater owners are very likely to pull the film before it finds its audience."

Finally, Peter has advice for guerilla marketing and indie filmmakers. "If an indie approach is determined, then narrow-focus on one or a few theaters, conduct a guerilla-style campaign for that film so that the theater is filled for days on end, and pray someone notices!"

PROMOTION: AN EXAMPLE IN MUSIC

You are the artist in the music industry looking for success. What advice do you receive if you are engaged in independent self-marketing in today's highly competitive business environment and the new entertainment industry paradigm?

Amanda Alexandrakis, President of Music and Promotion, Inc., is a seasoned professional in national radio promotion and marketing, and has this suggestion for the artist, whether he or she is emerging or already successful. "Without promotion, either on your own or with a professional organization, the project is doomed. If a band wants to play in their garage and not sell records or have fans, then that band is doing it as a hobby. If an artist is attempting to make it in the music business, then they will need to meticulously plot their promotion and marketing strategy and stick with it."

Amanda believes the successful band always has a strategy, putting a team together for each part of the project, including radio, press, booking, and touring. She states, "Education and networking are key elements. You must understand basic marketing. If a band says their music appeals to everyone, then that band needs serious help. Nothing appeals to everyone and every company has a demographic. Knowing basic business skills and learning industry standards is essential to success."

When it comes to a discussion of promotion in the new social media, Amanda has this to say. "It's absolutely necessary to use social media outlets to expose a band or an artist's music. If a band or artist does not have a Facebook or Twitter account, they are not perceived as a serious artist. There is no excuse why these avenues should not be exploited, as they are free. In addition, the amount of fans and industry contacts one can gain is invaluable."

In essence, heed the words of the experts and look to all of the opportunities you may find within social media. The applications can have enormous impact on the marketing of your career.

MARKETING RULES!

Marketing rules in the commercial world of the new entertainment industry.

Amanda tells us that practically all promotion in music is essentially marketing, commenting, "There are two areas in which an artist needs to focus. The first is finding fans. The more CDs you sell, the more friends you have on Facebook, the more followers on Twitter, and the more attention you will get. A smart band will leverage this into even more attention."

As to the second area in marketing, Amanda states, "Once a band gains a fan base and starts to show some success, they need to get their name known within the industry. The world of music is surprisingly small, and networking at industry functions is essential. Making yourself known to your local radio station, going to community music networking events, and making friends with other bands are all very important ways to get opportunities for your band. Once you get the support in your community, branch out statewide, then regionally."

However, as a caveat, Kim Kolback adds, "Guerilla marketing and social networks are introducing us to massive amounts of entertainment content, some of which is good and some of which is not so good. This means many more choices and the need for the consumer to sift through those choices. We may see more short-term celebrities as the result of aggressive social media and hype, and fewer long-term industry icons."

Los Angeles entertainment attorney and author Todd Brabec feels that one has to be involved with all of the social media to find success. "There is no way around it. There has to be some coordination of effort in using the media as to what you are putting out and what your message is. You must have a plan of action and not do things in a 'shotgun, willy-nilly fashion.' The plan also has to have some relationship to your efforts in the traditional media."

And Maryann Ridini Spencer does not want the artist to forget the importance of networking within the industry as part of a marketing plan, commenting, "It is essential to network, and that is something that takes time and patience. You may not even be aware of how you are building that network either. The best way to go about it is to always be pleasant, fair, and true to your word, and enjoy what you do. Help others when you can and get creative."

And so the business paradigm continues to spin and morph within the entertainment industry while you try to determine how to deal with it on the path toward recognition, critical acclaim, and success.

Yet however long and difficult the road is, it is well worth the trip.

INSTANT REPLAY

Ultimately, you must create your own industry paradigm, which will morph as the industry continues to develop, and which will include a comprehensive understanding of the world of promotion and marketing in order to implement your distribution plans. All the while, remember to continue to create great content, which is what your art should be all about.

AND IT'S A WRAP

And it's a wrap, with some thoughts for your consideration.

A basic knowledge of the business of entertainment is needed in order to further your career as an artist.

The new industry paradigm has been changing at an ever-increasing rate with the advent of digital technology and all content that lies within it. In this new digital frontier, there exists a subtle balance between artistry and commercialism.

Understanding this new paradigm may seem daunting. However, it is exciting and challenging and reflective of the new world of entertainment.

FILM

* The business of film requires a solid academic and practical understanding of the structure of the industry, including the nature of creating, investing in, producing, and distributing films.

* The new industry paradigm may vary depending on your position within the industry and your goals. However, the paradigm as a concept is very real and universal, and it will affect the manner in which everyone does business.

TELEVISION

* Television provides us with not only entertainment but news and information. Its business infrastructure is very competitive and welcomes innovative programming.

* Your understanding of the business of television is an essential part of finding success within that industry.

MUSIC

* Perhaps more so than in film or television, an understanding of the new distribution mechanisms inherent in music is essential to working successfully in the industry.

* Though it is relatively less expensive for an artist to record new music today, the marketing of music has become more complicated because of the new available avenues for digital distribution. At the same time,

opportunities are greater and show more promise for both the emerging and established artist.

THE LITERARY ARTS

★ The publishing industry, like the music industry, is searching for a new direction to define itself, and the issues of distribution and marketing are at the forefront.

★ Writers and publishers share many similar concerns about the sale of books and shrinking profit margins because of the rise of ebooks and Internet downloading. Yet as long as people read books, the industry will survive and prosper.

FASHION AND MODELING

★ The opportunities in fashion and modeling are there for any enterprising individual who understands the business rules of engagement.

★ These areas provide great opportunities for success by opening doors for new designers to look not only forward to tomorrow's couture style, but backward to vintage styles from the past to set today's new fashion standards.

THE VISUAL ARTS AND THE FINE ARTS

★ The visual arts and the fine arts have been less affected by the new distribution mechanisms, primarily because the distribution and sale of paintings and photographs are still primarily handled by gallerists and auction houses.

★ Yet the Internet plays an important new part in making such content available for sale, and that aspect of distribution is expanding.

LIGHTS, CAMERA, ACTION!

You have had a crash course in the business of the entertainment industry. For all this, you will need a team, and not just any team. You need an experienced team of professionals dedicated to your cause.

In the next chapter, you will be introduced to them as you continue along your career path toward success in the industry.

A STORY INSPIRED BY A COACH AND HIS DREAM

He had thought about it.

A story of a period in his life when he was a young coach and the world was still new.

He thought of the times when he would bundle himself up against the bitter cold of a Boston winter, driving to Cambridge Rindge and Latin High to lead his players in yet another game of basketball as they battled their way into the rankings and another championship season.

Years later, he would wonder if there was any sort of story to tell, and whether anyone would find it interesting or worth reading.

And he thought of the kids, the young athletes, many from broken and impoverished homes, who wanted to play basketball, starting first on the streets of Cambridge, Massachusetts, and working their way up the sports ladder to intermural games at the recreation center and then to middle school and high school.

These were kids who were predominantly African American and who saw hope and opportunity in a college education and sports, if only they could achieve that.

But they all had the same lofty goal: to be successful on the basketball court.

And with an incredible combination of hard work, practice, talent, and planning, he took his Cambridge Rindge and Latin Warriors to three consecutive state high school basketball championships with an astounding won-loss record of 77–1 over the course of three seasons.

He had gone on to coach other teams at other times, having coached at Boston University, George Washington University, and St. John's University, winning division titles and taking his teams to the NIT and NCAA, and then taking over the helm at Florida Atlantic University.

Nevertheless, though a million memories would come to mind about his career, he would always come back to his Warriors at Cambridge Rindge and Latin.

Those were the years when time stood still, life was forever, and tomorrow would always hold the promise of being better.

And one day, he decided to write a story about those times, a dramatic adaptation of how a coach and his team of very talented kids from Cambridge made basketball history.

So he began to write.

In his spare time, he sat at his desk, taking notes from all of the newspaper clippings he kept, recalling the names of his friends and other coaches with whom he had the pleasure of working.

He was introduced to an entertainment attorney, who then introduced him to an editor and a literary manager and writing coach, and his story began to unfold in the form of a treatment and screenplay. He worked very hard as he completed his drafts and revisions with professional guidance and editorial assistance.

And through it all, he remembered the kids.

This was, in reality, their story as much as his. They were the kings of their court.

So he gave the screenplay a working title: *Court of Kings*.

And he is the king of his court. He is the head coach of the Florida Atlantic University Owls, an NCAA Division I basketball team.

He is Coach Mike Jarvis.

And he is an artist.

THREE

YOU AND YOUR TEAM: MERGING YOUR ARTISTRY WITH THE INDUSTRY

What's with the blues, oh baby, what can you lose
Or maybe, you have forgotten how to dance
Great Rock 'N' Roll is buried deep in your soul
And when the jukebox starts to play
We'll dance away.

Richard Warren Rappaport, "Great Rock 'N' Roll,"
from the motion picture soundtrack of *Concert* and the
theme from *Hello Hollywood*

THE BASICS

This chapter is about merging your artistry with the entertainment industry and introduces your team in order to prepare for the journey ahead. The roles of your team members and their collective contributions to your career are discussed as you are advised and counseled on the path toward the attainment of artistic and commercial success.

Once in place, your team will primarily consist of the following members:

- ★ the entertainment attorney
- ★ the talent manager
- ★ the literary manager and writing coach
- ★ the agent
- ★ the editor
- ★ the producer
- ★ the publicist

The entertainment attorney is in many ways the team leader. The responsibilities of this individual are addressed, including the importance of providing sound legal advice in entertainment law and business and assisting you in arriving at the right decisions for your career.

The responsibilities of your other team members are discussed. The talent manager works with you to determine how certain aspects of your artistic future are managed. The literary manager and writing coach provides advice in all forms and styles of creative writing. The agent looks for opportunities to present you as an artist within the industry. The editor offers editorial oversight in conjunction with the literary manager. The producer is involved in creating and producing your project. The publicist assists you in all aspects of promotion, marketing, and public relations.

Lastly, the vital importance of strategizing with your entire team is discussed, along with the need to coordinate with each team member.

WHY THIS CHAPTER IS IMPORTANT TO YOU

Simply put, your team is there to advise you, direct you, and protect you in your climb to the top, regardless of the genre in which you work.

FILM

★ In the motion picture industry, whether you are a producer, director, cinematographer, music supervisor, screenwriter, actor, or any other individual involved in production, distribution, or marketing, your team can be indispensible.

★ Your team will provide you with the right expertise at the right time, in order to ensure a professional presentation within the industry and take a film project from your carpet to the red carpet.

TELEVISION

★ In the television industry, where many projects for broadcast are developed and produced relatively quickly, your team's expertise and professional skills can make the difference.

★ As in film, your team can be critical in taking a project from its inception to development and production.

MUSIC

★ Teamwork is what the music industry is all about. Your team is absolutely essential to you because development of an artist's career is where errors in artistic direction can sometimes move that career in the wrong direction.

★ As in all other fields in entertainment, whether you are a producer, engineer, artist, or any other individual dedicated to a project, the team must coordinate with you to "even the playing field" against the competition.

THE LITERARY ARTS

★ In the ever-changing landscape of the literary arts, publishers will expect you to have your team in place when the time comes for your work to be introduced to the business world.

★ Publishers are familiar with literary agents and entertainment attorneys, and your team will ensure that any publishing contracts will be properly and expeditiously handled.

FASHION AND MODELING

★ Your team can play a significant role in protecting your interests in fashion and modeling, where unknown designers or emerging models can become international figures overnight and change the face of the industry.

★ Once that happens, your talents and your team will take you to runways around the world, where the next great styles in fashion are born.

THE VISUAL ARTS AND FINE ARTS

★ Teamwork can make the difference to ensure that your artistic works are presented to the right galleries in the right cities at the right time.

★ Your art has the power to excite the world, and your team will help make it happen.

— THE COURT OF ARTISTIC OPINION —
"COUNSELORS, APPROACH THE BENCH"

You are wearing your best jeans and jacket (after all, you are the artist) and slowly open the doors to peer into the Court of Artistic Opinion. The courtroom is filling up, but court is not yet in session. Spectators are still waiting. A few turn around and look at you. You feel a little nervous. And you should. Your team is not with you yet. But that is going to change very quickly. You close the doors and straighten your jacket. It's "team time."

There is a great deal to do and now is the time to do it. So let's meet your team!

THE TEAM

It's time to rock with your team and hit the ground running.

As you begin your path to success, perhaps the most pivotal decision you will make is to pick the team that will best represent your interests in the entertainment industry. In this respect, you will be working with individuals who are skilled in their respective areas of expertise and dedicated to the achievement of your goals and aspirations. And if there is any time in your career when it is essential to surround yourself with those who are in a position to assist, it will be at the beginning, when opportunities are just starting to develop.

As with every other aspect of your career path, there is a financial cost to utilizing the services of the professionals who will make up your team.

You may believe such costs are beyond your budget, especially because you, like many other new artists, operate under a fairly strict budget, realizing you must be cognizant of your expenses in order to "remain in the game."

Yet the truth is that in most instances, there is a much greater cost to foregoing those professional services. The failure to proceed under the advice of an entertainment attorney and other experts on your team can lead to disastrous legal and business consequences, thereby jeopardizing, delaying, or even ruining a once promising career.

You may be surprised to find that most professionals on your team can work closely with you to assist in controlling fees and costs so you may have the benefit of their expertise and, at the same time, stay within your budget as you continue to develop your career.

Your entertainment attorney is on deck and waiting to go to bat for you.

THE ENTERTAINMENT ATTORNEY

The most important decision you may make at the beginning of your professional career is to have the advice and counsel of an experienced and qualified attorney in entertainment law.

Your attorney's expertise must include a solid understanding of the artistic and business aspects of the industry, as well as corporate law in general, with specific emphasis on those particular areas that pertain to your current and prospective interests.

THE ATTORNEY'S ROLE

The role of the entertainment attorney is absolutely critical in the development of your career.

Los Angeles entertainment attorney Dixon Q. Dern talks about the importance of the role of the entertainment attorney to the entire process of client representation in the industry. "Major artists usually have a critical team of representatives, including the attorney, the agent, the personal manager, and sometimes the public relations person."

Dixon places great emphasis on the need for good legal advice in that process. "The role of the attorney is indispensible to the entire team. The agent finds the deals and negotiates major terms, and the personal manager advises and consults as to the propriety of doing the deal. If the artist, manager, and agent decide the deal is doable, they will bring in the attorney, not only to have his or her opinion as to whether the deal should be done, but, of equal importance, to negotiate terms, review the contracts, and the like."

New York entertainment attorney Joseph Serling agrees. "As a lawyer, it is essential to strategize with your client throughout his or her career. Numerous legal issues come up, and it is critical for the client to have an entertainment attorney who is well versed in all the client's entertainment affairs."

Joe emphasizes the importance of continued representation and the need for constant contact. "The attorney is one of the only people who will have the client's best interests at heart. In many situations, the client will permit other parties in his or her 'camp' to become the link between the client and the attorney. This is a huge mistake by the client, who should maintain a direct relationship with the entertainment lawyer."

Ft. Lauderdale and Nashville entertainment attorney John F. Bradley concurs and adds, "To be the most effective, an entertainment attorney must have an absolute understanding of the functioning of the industry, its internal relationships, and the workings of its highly complicated contracts."

And Atlanta entertainment attorney Joseph Arrington II remarks, "With the emergence of new technologies and innovations, it is increasingly important that clients seek an entertainment attorney. These new technologies not only require legal analyses but also provide a platform for reaching a network of individuals who are the new tastemakers for the industry. In this regard, the value of an entertainment attorney is in providing networking as well as being available for ongoing consultations with the client."

Your entertainment attorney should become your trusted legal advisor and may be the crucial link between the development of your art and commercial success. As you read on, you will understand the importance of having your attorney assist you in your efforts to move forward toward artistic and commercial success.

SOUND LEGAL ADVICE AND THE OPPORTUNITIES FOR SUCCESS

Why is sound legal advice important to you in finding success?

Entertainment attorney and author Todd Brabec states his reasons very succinctly. "Contracts, license agreements, and legal advice, both before and after events, are a part of practically every aspect of an artist's career. In today's world of multiple platforms, new media, and changing business models, the opportunities for success are at an all-time high." Based on that, Todd feels that success needs to be tempered by the fact that the consequences of one's actions, both on legal grounds and in a business or financial sense, can be more significant than ever before, commenting, "The attorney is there to protect a client in every aspect of his or her career, as well as to advise and to warn."

New York entertainment attorney George N. Stein emphasizes his reasons, particularly at the start of an artist's career, believing that strong legal representation is especially important at both the early "development" stage and later when the client is established. "Strong representation at the early stages of a career is important because it is often in those early stages that the 'cornerstone' deals are made, such as management, recording, publishing, song collaboration, producing, and band partnerships, among other things. These are the kinds of deals that impact careers for years, for better or worse."

When clients become better known or even famous, the deals will obviously become larger monetarily. George feels that will require the close attention of the attorney. "In this respect, an experienced entertainment attorney will be able to leverage the artist's increased stature into stronger and more lucrative deals."

The issues that you will face during this aspect of your career may seem very complicated and at times difficult to understand. Your entertainment attorney should have the ability to speak clearly to you on these matters and make them understandable so that you may make the right decisions for your future.

THE IMPORTANCE OF ACCESS TO YOUR ENTERTAINMENT ATTORNEY
When is the time right for you to have access to your entertainment attorney?

Entertainment attorney Kim Kolback stresses the importance of access. "It is not simply to educate the artist about the industry. It is to keep the artist out of undesirable contractual relations and provide sound career advice relating to the everyday needs of the artist, such as problematic publicity, blogging, promotions, statements, branding, protecting of intellectual rights, estate planning, and other matters."

New York entertainment attorney Paul LiCalsi also discusses access. "While the manager, business manager, or agent each have important roles, the entertainment lawyer is often involved in all aspects of the artist's career and can be the central advisor for the artist in dealing with each of these other representatives."

YOUR ATTORNEY'S EXPERTISE WITHIN THE INDUSTRY

The expertise your entertainment attorney provides can act as a foundation for you on your path to success. He or she may advise you on relevant and current industry standards and practices as they relate to your field. Coupled with that, your attorney should possess a level of skill in contracts and other transactional matters and negotiations.

This will include the knowledge to observe and follow proper protocol when making pertinent industry contacts as well as solid knowledge and experience in business law and all aspects of intellectual property law, including trademarks, service marks, and copyrights.

Other important skills that are needed will also relate to alternative dispute resolution, or ADR, which deals with handling and settling disputes between or among parties to a contract in order to avoid litigation. Such alternatives to a suit are preferred for several reasons. From a purely financial perspective, the cost of litigation can be astronomical, whereas alternative dispute resolution is much less expensive. From a practical standpoint, the avoidance of litigation can be significant to your career, because lawsuits often make the press, which, from a public relations standpoint, may not necessarily be helpful to your cause in the entertainment industry.

And if your lawyer has experience in ADR, it is very likely he or she will have litigation experience or will be able to refer you to an experienced litigator who will act as co-counsel if the situation warrants. That will be beneficial to you because experience in the courtroom and in law and procedure relating to litigation will permit the attorney to know what steps to take to avoid litigation pitfalls when drafting agreements.

THE LAWYER AS A COUNSELOR ON YOUR PROJECTS

Your entertainment attorney may be a sounding board for projects you wish to pursue as an artist.

Entertainment attorney Emily Graham states, "Practically all art is subject to critique. When you are the writer who tells me that your story is quite possibly the very best in the world, I will tell you as diplomatically as possible that there's no accounting for taste. So please don't be upset if I don't say your screenplay is the most brilliant or commercially appealing piece I have ever seen. However, I will applaud your efforts in making the attempt to write it and share your story with the world."

Your attorney may also inform you when it is not quite the time to seek his or her advice. Emily comments, "I recall when a very fine musician, who was planning his band's upward ascent within the industry, asked me if it was necessary to have a lawyer available every step of the way for success. My answer was that, while, at that particular moment, they did not need a lawyer, they did need to tour and develop a following. So when a contract is presented, the lawyer should always be available."

And your lawyer can provide you with advice not only on what you think about, but what you do not think about.

Entertainment attorney Peter Dekom weighs in on some of the nuts-and-bolts issues that people don't consider in entertainment that can make or break a project, based on a failure to seek competent legal counsel beforehand. "When film and television producers attempt to 'save money' in deciding not to seek counsel on legal work, such as clearances, chain-of-title, insurance, and the need to comply with securities laws, they wind up incurring enormous fees they will have to pay to lawyers later to undo the mess they created."

Peter provides the perfect example of what you should not be doing in this regard. "A film that is a mess cannot be distributed, so if you really want to destroy the tiniest vestige of commercial viability, blissfully dance into the work of failing to withhold taxes, not getting precisely the correct contracts at precisely the right moments from precisely the right people, skip insurance (even statutorily required workers compensation), and use unpaid 'interns' who are not part of an established 'for-credit' academic program."

And that's not all. Peter discusses a few more things you should be doing that you may forget to do. You may fail to clear people in the shot or anyone who does anything creative for the film, fail to clear every bit of music you use, fail to get every conceivable right to any material you are using in precisely the correct way, fail to comply with the law when raising money, fail to get errors and omissions insurance, or fail to understand that there is no such thing as a 'fair use' defense when you step on someone else's copyright. If you make these mistakes, prepare to buy some young lawyer the Mercedes-Benz he or she has been drooling over, and not the C class!

Your attorney may be your best defense against costly errors, omissions, or other mistakes that can slow your path toward success or even derail your career. Listen to your lawyer. Knowledge is everything, and you can never really have enough. There is always more to learn. And life, especially in the entertainment industry, involves a constant learning curve.

THE ATTORNEY'S FEES

As with all the members of your team, an important discussion must be had with your attorney at the outset of representation relating to how he or she will be compensated. In this regard, you must also have an understanding with your attorney for services rendered concerning charges for time and out-of-pocket costs so that you are able to control such expenses.

There are general rules you should expect when dealing with prospective fees from your attorney and professional fees from other team members. Most attorneys will charge for their representation by the hour. However, your attorney may be willing to work with you at a very low hourly rate, a reduced or flat monthly rate, a percentage of your gross earnings, a deferred rate, or no rate at all for a period of time, depending on the particular circumstances.

When you do have an understanding with your attorney as to representation, he or she will present you with a retainer agreement, which will outline the nature of representation and compensation. Though a full discussion of such agreements is beyond the scope of this chapter, you should carefully review that agreement with your attorney prior to signing it so that you fully understand its contents.

Once retained, your attorney can play an invaluable role in your successful climb to the top, and he or she can become not only your trusted advisor but also, in some instances, your mentor. And as mentioned earlier in this chapter, your attorney can assist you in negotiating fee agreements or other arrangements with the remaining members of your team so that you will have the financial staying power to push forward in your career and focus your efforts on finding success.

Remember that you are also a member of your team. Your cooperation as a team player will enable your lawyer to have the opportunity to provide the best advice across the board, including when you do or do not need legal services, as well as when you need to be thinking about issues that are critical to your future. Thus, when speaking to your attorney, take careful notes and be very attentive, because you will find that you can learn a great deal just by listening. In this respect, do not forget that mistakes in the entertainment industry accomplish two things: first, your reputation as an artist may be damaged, and, second, you may spend much more on your project than you intended by not obtaining professional advice. And time is an invaluable resource, not to be wasted.

The success of your career may very well depend on the advice you receive from your lawyer as well as the other members of your team. So be aware and informed.

INSTANT REPLAY

The entertainment attorney's role on your team is critical to your success. Continual access to your attorney is essential. You must regard your lawyer as a counselor and advocate, remembering that the advice you will receive is not only what you think about, but what you do not think about.

THE TALENT MANAGER

A talent manager has expertise in all aspects of the management of your artistic affairs, including personal management, permitting you to focus on the development of your career.

TALENT MANAGEMENT

What is entailed in talent management in general, and why does an artist need such personal management?

Producer Maryann Ridini Spencer, who is also a talent manager, states, "As talent managers, we specialize in working with clients in creating a unified and powerful identity with desired objectives and goals, as we work in tandem with their agents and other members of their team."

Maryann also talks about what her clients want the most from her services. "It is very important to provide advice and counsel with respect to general entertainment industry practices, such as assistance with the selection of literary and artistic material and assistance in all business matters related to a client's career, including public relations, marketing, photography, résumés, videos, and web sites. It is also important to provide advice on compensation, privileges, and amenities in conjunction with advice from the client's agent and attorney. In short, we do whatever is necessary to foster an artist's career."

Your talent manager can be the individual who creates success for you in your career as an artist. His or her guidance is absolutely essential in this regard.

INDUSTRY CONTACTS

How important are the contacts that your talent manager will make for you within the entertainment industry?

They are critical. For example, in music, your manager will build solid, deep-rooted relationships with the operators of the various performance venues so that you can cut the best contractual deals, including an assurance that you will be properly compensated for your efforts. In essence, your manager becomes a trusted advisor so that you can be apprised of everything, thus enabling you to make decisions that will place your career in the best light and play to your strengths.

This is especially true given that your manager is attempting to take your talent to the marketplace, make the proper introductions, and open the proper doors so the world can see what you have to offer.

MANAGING YOUR FUTURE

And what of the manager's ability to look into the future and understand, evaluate, and define your path to success?

Maryann Ridini Spencer comments, "From a manager's standpoint, you must start by knowing yourself. In other words, know your weaknesses and strengths and where you can best help the artist. You must recognize that there are certain individuals who have incredible talent and those who do not, or who need further study and practice at their craft before moving forward professionally. So you have to distinguish among these possibilities, and sometimes you have to take a pass on representation."

Richard Willis Jr. is a writer, producer, director, manager, and CEO and executive producer of Mozell Entertainment Group, New York City. Richard also speaks to this issue, commenting, "To be a manager is to be part of a new artist's future and the discovery that he or she is an artist, at whatever their craft may be, then formulating a strategy on how they may sustain themselves within their craft."

Never underestimate the influence and importance of your manager. He or she can be a valuable asset on your road to success.

THE TALENT MANAGER'S FEES

What types of fees should you expect to pay a manager?

To begin, most talent managers operate on a commission basis and do not require fees in advance, other than costs associated with their representation.

On such fees in general, Maryann Ridini Spencer states, "In film and television, talent managers customarily receive a 25 percent commission, while agents receive 10 percent. And talent managers do not negotiate monies paid to clients. That is generally done by the agent or attorney."

Similarly, in other genres managers will expect commissions from 15 to 25 percent for their management.

Needless to say, you should consult with your attorney when

choosing a manager to represent you. You should also have your attorney review any talent management contract prior to signing it in order to ensure that the agreement conforms to current industry standards and practices. Your attorney will also negotiate any revisions of that agreement when necessary.

INSTANT REPLAY

Your talent manager will help guide you along the path of your chosen career as an artist. Your manager can provide you with very valuable industry contacts and will help prepare you for your future as an artist.

THE LITERARY MANAGER AND WRITING COACH

Your literary manager, who may also be a writing coach, can become one of your greatest allies in your quest for success within the entertainment industry.

This individual is an experienced industry representative and insider who works with writers in all genres of the literary arts so that they may develop their careers as novelists or screenwriters. The literary manager assists both creatively—through consultations on story development, time management, and creating priorities—and financially—through assisting in the marketing of the writer's product. The value of such a diverse background cannot be underestimated. Moreover, the literary manager, unlike the agent, has the ability to produce in all aspects of the entertainment industry.

Though you may think that the literary manager deals only in literary matters, such as manuscripts or screenplays, you will find that the level of expertise is far more encompassing and will generally include knowledge of all aspects of motion pictures and television as well as music in film and television. Therefore, it is highly advisable that as an artist in the new entertainment industry, you utilize the services of a literary manager, either on a regular basis or as needed.

The literary manager can provide advice and guidance at a time in your career when you need it most.

CONTENT IS KING

In many ways, writing is what it is all about in the entertainment industry, where content is king! And that is where the literary manager comes in.

Producer and literary manager Ken Atchity states, "I've spent my lifetime writing and working with and for writers, as a career coach, editor, publisher, producer, literary manager, and public speaker. I've weathered the ups and downs of the entertainment, publishing, and Internet industries, but one thing has remained consistent: writers are the ones who provide content. And content, which we can also call 'information' or 'stories,' is what the world has an insatiable appetite for."

SUCCESSFUL PROJECTS AND GREAT STORIES

Many in Hollywood emphatically state that writers rule in the film and television industries. Creative writing is all about the need for great stories, and in the entertainment industry we are always speaking about creating such stories.

Ken believes in the incredible power of such stories. When

asked once what it is that makes a great story, he replied, "A great story is a story that moves the reader to delight, to action, and to thought. It has strong characters and a strong beginning, middle, and end. I am a content facilitator and a career coach who helps writers who are content providers with the strategy and tactics required to get their work in front of the public in the most expeditious and most productive way possible, given the changing times in which we live."

One of Ken's companies is The Story Merchant, which is the entity under which he can provide direct, one-on-one coaching in writing. The Writer's Lifeline is the company he supervises to provide editorial and ghostwriting services from a select team of writers and editors, and his literary management company, Atchity Entertainment International, Inc., is involved in motion picture and television production.

Ken also discusses time management for the artist in the world of creative writing and the arts, claiming, "The only way to make your dreams within the industry come true is to manage your goals, such as getting your film or television project out of development and into preproduction and focusing on your objectives. For instance, getting your storyline straight and finding a director."

Your literary manager and writing coach will also be important in assisting you in maintaining an agenda in moving toward your project goals.

In this respect, Ken suggests you should periodically try to schedule time to examine and, if necessary, reschedule your goals, writing a list of priorities and giving each a deadline. This will permit you to maintain greater control over your time and make the decision process easier. "By reminding yourself of what you've accomplished, you can keep your head together and succeed in managing your time. And by managing your time, you can manage your life. For while knowledge may be regarded as constituting power in Hollywood, time is the lifeblood of most successful players."

Regardless of your type and style of artistry, your time is critically important and cannot be measured just in hours, days, and months. It is measured by the quality of your artistic output. So you must make your time count and regard it as one of your most valuable assets.

THE LITERARY MANAGER'S FEES

Your literary manager may work with you on a commission basis, although there are times when he or she may work on an hourly or per-project basis, especially if it relates to work of an editorial nature.

With regard to commissions, although most successful literary managers charge 15 percent, fees are subject to negotiation depending on the nature of the project and other relevant circumstances, and are generally based on current industry standards and practices and protocol in the entertainment industry.

It is best to have your attorney analyze, review, and negotiate the literary manager's contract on your behalf. Once retained, the literary manager will work closely with the rest of your team to assist you on your path to success.

> **INSTANT REPLAY**
>
> Your literary manager can be essential to your success, providing advice in the creation of written content and assisting in branding you within your chosen field.

THE AGENT

Agents are the representatives of talent, both domestically and internationally. And they can create a stellar career for talent. Agents represent actors, novelists, screenwriters, songwriters, musicians, vocalists, music producers, film producers, television producers, theatrical producers, directors, public speakers, and anyone involved in any capacity in the creative arts. In essence, agents are at the heart of the entertainment industry.

THE IMPORTANCE OF THE AGENCY PROCESS

How important are agents?

An agent may permit you to climb to the highest levels of success in the industry.

Author Carolina Garcia-Aguilera finds that agents are critical to her accomplishments as a writer, emphatically stating, "I am a firm believer in the agency process. And you need an agent with whom you are compatible on literary, artistic, and business levels, and who thoroughly understands the genre in which you write."

In her world of creative writing, Carolina tells us that the agent will be the one who has the power to persuade an editor to stand behind your property. Lamenting the days when the editor could make that decision unilaterally, Carolina feels that today the editor must at least bring the property to the attention of the agent and others in "corporate" who have the ability to make the decision to "green light" the project.

THE NEED FOR AGENCY REPRESENTATION

Agency representation is ciritcal to long-term success.

Pat Quinn is a prominent former literary agent and considered one of the finest in Hollywood, combining years of experience with vast knowledge of the industry. Pat is now president of Quinn Media Management in Beverly Hills and has advised companies around the world as a special media consultant.

Speaking about emerging creative writers, Pat underscores the absolute need for agency representation and also expresses the need for a writer to be focused and entrepreneurial in order to become successful. "Get a short of your movie made. Put something representative of your voice up on YouTube. Take advantage of our amazing technology and start getting your work produced. It will be much easier to introduce your vision through a two-minute short over the Internet than through a written script."

Ken Atchity also comments on the importance of agents as individuals who are part of the process in securing deals in film and television, stating, "In Hollywood, I sometimes work with agents as packagers or co-representatives."

SEEKING REPRESENTATION

When seeking agency representation, you must realize that most agencies will not accept submissions directly from an artist for any works that are not solicited, nor will they accept submissions from individuals who do not have such representation. So how does one secure an agent? Through a team! They will be in the best position to use their contacts, influence, and introductions to find you an agent who is suitable for your career needs.

Often your entertainment attorney can be the one who opens that door, or your personal manager, talent manager, or literary manager may make such introductions. Another possibility is that some agents may follow your career as an emerging artist, preparing for the day when you are ready to develop professionally. Regardless, it is the personal contact that will serve to open the door to consideration for agency representation.

Once you are signed by an agent, he or she will also work closely with the rest of your team on your career development and the presentation of your work within the industry.

YOUR TALENTS AND ABILITIES

It is important to remember that your agent will take you on as a client based on your talents and abilities. Thus, regardless of the contacts used to get such representation, the commencement of that representation is just the beginning. In the entertainment industry, every day is important, and it is often said that you are only as good as the success of your last project.

Ken Atchity provides a caveat as to what an artist may reasonably expect of his or her agent. He explains that though the artist should be getting attention, feedback, and sales action from the agent, this is not typically the case. "The sheer reality of an agent's life means that he or she must focus on projects that bring in income." Thus, in order to find yourself at the top of your agent's "A" list, you should expect to spend a great deal of time developing your artistic works in order to build your reputation as an artist who can make money.

Once you have representation, give your agent the best that you can with your talent, skills, and ambition in order to climb to the top, find success, and remain there.

THE AGENT'S FEES

As a general rule, your agent will typically work on a commission basis, averaging about 10 or 15 percent of your earnings from the deal or project in which you are placed.

Of course, any agency representation agreement should be carefully evaluated by your attorney and discussed with you to be certain that it conforms with current industry practices and that the agent has the capability to make at least reasonable efforts to assist you in your career.

INSTANT REPLAY
Your agent has the ability to present you to the world. The agency process, involving interaction with practically every important individual or company in your industry, can be invaluable to your artistic and professional affairs.

THE EDITOR
Regardless of the area of the entertainment industry in which you find yourself, it is highly likely that you will need the services of a personal editor who is engaged in the professional revisions of your

written works, in order to ensure that the content you create is prepared in accordance with the industry standards within your field. Any person submitting a written work—such as a novel, article, screenplay, treatment, synopsis, or presentation of any sort—needs an editor. In fact, editors are needed for practically all written content, regardless of the nature of your artistry.

THE FUNCTIONS OF AN EDITOR

What are the editor's functions?

Editor Kate Burgauer is the president of Compass Rose Creative Services and a professional creative writing editor and screenwriter. "Your editor will conduct a review of your written documents for form and grammar, and will also suggest story and character ideas to improve the overall work. If you have a creative product that you want to sell, you should show it to an editor who can help you make it the absolute best that it can be."

Your editor should have professional credentials in creative writing. This field is typically studied in college as part of an undergraduate degree in communications or film. Creative writing is very specialized and includes understanding the concept of writing and story structure. For novelists and screenwriters, the editor will provide direction, oversight, advice, and hands-on editing to deal with the proper creation and structure of content.

AN EXAMPLE IN THE LITERARY ARTS: THE STORY ARC AND PLOT

Your editor should assist you in defining important structural elements of your written work. A story arc is generally a storyline that has episodic structure and exists in dramatic pieces, whether fictional or based on a true story, in film, television, or books. The story arc is used to illustrate movement of a character from one emotional state to another, and thus change, such as moving from happiness to sadness and back again, or from weakness to strength.

Structure in a story should be dramatic. The plot is a combination of the events within a story in their entirety in order to reach or achieve a specific creative and artistic effect, providing the reader or viewer with the theme of that story.

Kate Burgauer states, "When I work with novelists, I like to make sure that the writer is using a well-formed outline. The outline keeps the story and writer on track. An outline is also a great tool for working chapter by chapter." Kate feels that the outline should be easy to review and should indicate how to fix holes in the plot or correct character discrepancies. She also believes that it is very important to make sure that the writer of a novel knows the genre in which the book will be categorized.

In this regard, Kate often likes to put this question to a writer: "Which section of the store do you see your book in at a major book chain?" The answer to that question helps the writer focus on the point of view, style, tone, and length of the novel.

THE GREAT AMERICAN SCREENPLAY

What is Kate's advice on creating that great American screenplay?

She suggests, "A well-crafted screenplay that tells an engaging story always begins with a well-written outline. Screenplays have so many changes of scene and location that the outline needs to be thought through very carefully. The outline stage of a screenplay will also make plot problems obvious."

Kate feels that if the main characters in the story arc are not interesting, it will reflected in the outline. "When it comes to the writing stage of the screenplay, visual descriptions are key. The scene details should be short, well written, and to the point. Dialogue should be realistic and entertaining and it must move the story forward. A screenplay must have story-driven dialogue to keep it interesting for the audience. And last but not least, all scenes should show something new about a character and move the plot forward. Kate remarks, "If the scene does not accomplish this, cut it!"

Kate believes that your editor must have the capacity to bring your information and content to the entire world with energy, guts, and power. And in our competitive artistic environment, that is a must, which raises an important question: What is it that makes a story compelling and worthy of reading? Once again, Kate provides direction, explaining that compelling stories have three very important elements.

First, the story must have characters to which an audience can relate. The characters can have flaws and problems, but a reader must be able to identify with them, especially the main characters.

Second, the story must have unique settings and situations. The settings can be anywhere from an oil field in Iraq to the bingo room in a nursing home. And the compelling quality arises from the way the setting and situations are described and used. Kate tells us that some of her favorite movies have a simple setting, but it is the world of the film, with its use of color, texture, and cinematography, that can make the scene unique.

Third, the story must have realistic dialogue and plot. Realism doesn't have to be boring and mundane. Telling a realistic story means using what the audience knows of the world around us as a basis for the dialogue and events within the story. Some of the most believable stories are set in fantasy worlds, but the conflicts, discussions, and story points could be happening right down your street.

Kate feels this quality makes the story real and accessible.

EXCELLENT WRITING AND EDITING

Excellent writing is what success can be all about in the entertainment industry.

Producer Daniel de Liege comments on how he would advise an aspiring screenwriter who wants to become successful. His answer is enlightening, based on years of experience in reading screenplays for consideration for the big screen. "Learn how to accept rejection and never quit! Seriously, it's a tough business. There are literally thousands of screenplays floating around all over Hollywood and New York, so the competition is very tough."

Daniel also remarks, "The best advice I can give writers is to hone your craft. Read books on writing screenplays. Take writing classes and of course, write often. Don't be afraid of criticism. It's the only way you are going to get better. Read completed screenplays from movies you like. That will help you see why you liked it and will show you how to better craft a character or a scene."

Writer Lauren Morris agrees, and relies on her editor. "The editor for me is my personal guide to creative writing. From developing the texture of the characters and the storyline to re-reading the final copy, my editor is the one person that I count on to give me a professional and unbiased opinion as to the quality of my work."

And creative writing does not stop in the world of screenwriting or prose. It also exists in a different form in practically every type of written content that is creative, original, and dynamic. For example, in music, the editor may even be important in assisting the artist in the creation of storylines within lyrics to a song.

The same is true for public speaking about your art. If you are beginning your career within the industry and plan to speak at an event or promote a specialized project such as an independent film or theatrical play, you would probably need assistance from an editor in preparing your outline or speech. In essence, a fine editor is highly recommended, regardless of what your genre is within the entertainment industry.

In the world of television, producer, broadcaster, and on-air personality René Katz of *Hello Hollywood*, now on iStudioi.com, has written extensively for her series. Her advice to young entrepreneurial producers in television is to always have either an editor or assistant producer with editorial skills to review your copy. "You always want to develop and support your ideas and concepts in order to bring original thoughts to television, especially those that have meaning and significance. The last thing you want as a writer, regardless of the content or to whom it is directed, is to use copy that does not measure up to professional standards."

So as not to underestimate the importance of writing and editing, it is imperative to realize that you will ultimately be responsible for your work. Therefore, you have an obligation to your team and to yourself to have your editor review and approve all such content.

THE EDITOR'S FEES

In general, editors may set charges on a per-project basis but will normally charge an hourly rate for their services. Such rates can vary significantly, depending on the scope and nature of the project, ranging from $25 per hour to hundreds of dollars per hour or a flat fee.

Always seek the advice of your attorney when presented with a contract for editorial work, in order to negotiate the necessary terms and conditions and the best rate to fit your budget.

Your editor will be critical to your success for anything that you create in the form of the written word, either as content constituting a direct interpretation of your works or providing an explanation of those works.

And that type of assistance is absolutely essential in your ascent into the industry.

INSTANT REPLAY

Your editor's involvement may be crucial to your success and can ensure that your writings, whether they relate directly to your work or otherwise, will best reflect your presence in the industry.

THE PRODUCER

Your producer is the individual who packages and presents a project, regardless of the genre, for development and production within any aspect of the entertainment industry in motion pictures, television, music, theater, and all of the arts.

THE WORLD OF PRODUCING

Producing takes an incredible amount of energy and focus.

René Katz poses the question, "What should a producer expect when going into a taping? Expect the unexpected! In other words, remember that once the cameras are rolling, there's no turning back. So do your 'show prep.'"

Artistic director Diana Lozano discusses the world of producing. "Although I love to perform, I often find myself getting into all aspects of production. From lighting and costume design to direction and choreography, one has to understand the entire creative process." Diana explains that she was academically prepared for this direction. "Oddly enough, my master's degree from Cal Arts is literally called Integrated Media, through the Schools of Performance Art, Design, Technology, and Management. Upon graduating, it became quickly clear that it was not going to be easy to find work in such a specialized field, so I ended up carving my own path."

Daniel de Liege speaks about producing as part of a team, explaining that it is the producer's vision that will in many ways define and direct the efforts of the team. "We make movies that make a difference. We are working on an alliance with other like-minded production companies to control our own destiny through financing, development, production, marketing, and distribution of our own product."

Similarly, your producer will work very closely with the other members of your team to ensure the greatest likelihood of success of your projects and your career.

A WORTHY PROJECT

What makes a producer's project worthy of success?

Daniel states, "The story. It's all about the story. For instance, at Prelude, we love underdog stories. For some reason, and not by design, we have a lot of sports stories in the pipeline. They tend to exude a lot of heart."

Maryann Ridini Spencer speaks about her vision of a worthy project in film and television production, describing how the key players are involved. "Depending upon the project, a producer's job can vary. In television, creative producers are writers and sometimes creators of their projects. In either episodic television or movies for television, there is often a line producer, who oversees the day-to-day work on the set. In film, the above may also be the case, but more often than not, producers in film oversee every element of the project, from optioning a property to development, financing, casting, and selecting the crew, as well as distribution and marketing. A producer in film is also responsible for overseeing the project's budget and serving as a liaison with studio executives."

Maryann makes it a point to work with projects she has optioned and takes an active role in every aspect of the production of the project. "Since it sometimes can take a while to mount a project, I've made a commitment to myself to only focus on those projects I write that are dear to my heart and for which I am passionate. It can take time to see a project make it to the screen since so much can come into play. I've discovered that for myself, I work best as a producer and writer, and sometimes even director." Maryann states that she feels it is essential that a producer know about every job function on a production.

Your producer can be the key for success within the entertainment industry, regardless of the type or style of production. And often you will have the opportunity to work with more than one producer, because as the artist, you will be in front of or behind the camera on different occasions for different projects.

THE PRODUCER'S FEES

Producers are typically paid by the production company, studio, or network and not by the artist, unless the artist is involved in some financial aspect of producing the project or is actually funding it.

Because each project is different, a producer's fees should be examined by your attorney in order to determine if the fee structure meets your budget.

Of course, your attorney should review any agreement presented by a producer to ascertain that the document conforms to current industry standards and practices, and to ensure that your interests are protected.

> ### INSTANT REPLAY
> Producers can define your works and present you artistically within the marketplace. Choosing a producer may be one of the most important decisions of your career. Make it a wise one and seek the advice of your attorney and other team members.

THE PUBLICIST

The importance of the publicist truly comes into play as you begin your ascent in the entertainment industry.

Your publicist will act to create, deal with, and manage publicity for you in public life. The publicist's challenge is to present information about a client in order to assist that client in moving forward in career development. Therefore, the publicist will often communicate with the press in creating or responding to coverage by the media.

Publicists, like many attorneys and agents, work in private practice representing numerous clients. Publicists also tend to focus on their particular expertise in the industry, such as the representation of actors, producers, or writers. Your publicist should have the requisite skills and personal contacts to handle your interests properly and to deal with problems that may arise.

THE PUBLICIST AS A PROMOTER

New York and Florida publicist Gina Franano speaks of the importance of retaining an experienced publicist within the industry. Gina discusses the role she envisions on behalf of her clients not only as a publicist, but also as a promoter. "Promotion should start immediately. Publicists get paid for all the things that they do, including name dropping, where appropriate."

However, Gina feels that if a client is multifaceted as a talent, as most are, the publicist will be required to branch out into other artistic areas. "Promotion must begin immediately in order to lock in the 'storylines' that others may not yet see about an artist and all that he or she does. You must be very creative in order for your client to be mentioned in so many different areas of the arts."

One of Gina's clients is Bon Jovi drummer Tico Torres. "I worked on branding Tico as a renaissance man because he was not only an accomplished professional musician, performing since he was 13 years old, but also because he is a very fine visual artist. He had always wanted to be successful as a painter as well as a businessman and philanthropist, and wanted to be branded properly." Gina assisted Tico in creating exhibits for his art, and after Tico sang with Bon Jovi on a Christmas album, Gina felt it was a good time to present him as a vocalist. She helped create a special concert with the late great Celia Cruz and Angelica Maria in Miami. There, Tico sang and played drums to a sold-out audience.

In the world of fashion, Gina assisted Tico when he began to learn about that field while married to model and spokesperson Eva Herzigova. Later, Tico designed clothes for his son under the commercially successful label Rock Star Baby.

Tico also loves to play golf, finding that it relaxes him in between concert tours. Gina remarks that once he began to play in tournaments, he realized that he could use the game to benefit charitable causes, and she assisted him in raising money for children through the Tico Torres Children's Foundation. Gina states, "All artists should evolve, just as Tico has. Artists should be using their emerging and existing celebrity toward projects or causes, charitable or otherwise, to better their lives and the lives of those around them. And the publicist should be the 'go-to' person to help develop that side of the artist."

UNDERSTANDING PUBLIC RELATIONS AND MARKETING

Maryann Ridini Spencer underscores the importance of being aware of the publicist's job. Although primarily a writer and producer, she feels that as part of that job description, it is essential to know how public relations and marketing work. "For me, having a production as well as a PR/marketing background has been a blessing. Today, more than ever, a producer must have a well-rounded

PR/marketing education because of how the media works and how information is received due to the technical advancements and the Internet and social media."

Maryann always educates her clients on the workings of the PR/ marketing machine and also suggests that clients or producers take a course in this field at a local college or online. In fact, many press release distribution houses offer free online courses in public relations and the new social media.

THE PUBLICIST'S FEES

Publicists do not typically work on a commission or contingency fee, but will generally charge for their services on a monthly basis under a retainer. For an artist emerging within the industry, the services of a publicist can be expensive. However, many publicists will negotiate with you to secure your representation, especially if they believe in you and your work and envision a future for you.

As always, have your attorney evaluate any retainer agreements presented to you by a publicist to ensure they conform to current industry standards and practices. And if your budget requires it, your attorney can assist you in attempting to negotiate a waiver or suspension of fees for an initial period of time.

Your publicist may be one of the professionals on your team with whom you will be working on practically a daily basis. The publicist's work can be critical to enhancing your reputation by putting out those sudden fires that can damage a career or even stop it in its tracks during tough times, and by spreading the word about your successes during good times.

> ### INSTANT REPLAY
>
> Your publicist can be vital to your career by informing the industry of your success and assisting you in handling press you may not want or need. All great publicists understand marketing, promotion, and public relations. Work closely with your publicist in order to evaluate and determine the best direction to take along your career path.

YOUR TEAM IS IN PLACE

In assembling your team, you have chosen to draw upon the expertise of several individuals who are highly qualified in their respective areas. Now it is time for you to begin to bring your team together so that they may work closely with you to assist you in achieving your goals. To accomplish this, you must engage in comprehensive strategizing with your team on your career path.

THE TEAM IS EVERYTHING

Your team will be a sounding board for strategizing as you plan your career ascent. They will assist you in mapping out plans for future success. You should be aware of all the steps being taken by members of your team on your behalf, and you should also make every attempt to understand specifically what each member of your team is doing and why.

In this manner, you can begin to learn the business and legal aspects of your industry as it specifically relates to your career.

GO TEAM!

Your team should be all about the right way for you to find success.

Recording artist, actor, and producer Aaron Carter states, "As an artist it is so important to have the right team around you. I compare my team to a house and its foundation. Without a solid foundation, the house would not be sturdy, would not have a good support and will most likely fall down and crumble. My team creates a great foundation for my career to keep it steadily growing in whatever direction I take. A strong team will get the artist's vision and in turn that allows me to grow both creatively and as an overall brand."

Author Steve Alten emphasizes the importance of his team. "They include my literary agent, who handles both foreign and domestic sales; my editor for feedback; my webmaster, who puts out my monthly newsletter; my artist, who does amazing work; my Facebook coordinator, who is helping build an Internet fan base; and the volunteers at Adopt-An-Author and my nonprofit teen reading program. For movie deals, I work with a producer, and my attorneys join in when there is a studio deal."

Psychologist and performance enhancement consultant Dr. Andrea Corn, PsyD, agrees. "Individually and collectively, the individuals comprising your team are in very important roles, although such roles are discrete and separate. Yet each player is essential in shaping, developing, and maintaining an artist's longevity. Before the artist can even plan a future, he or she must ask what is going on in the here and now."

Jean (Jeannie) Landfair Enright began her career on the set of Starz's *Magic City*. "My team provides guidance and support; especially my sister, Shayla, who has always been an inspiration to me."

Director, screenwriter, and actor Victoria Ann Parker discusses the importance of the team approach, stating, "It's critical to have a strategy as an emerging artist, and a great relationship with each of your colleagues is a must. I am just beginning to observe others who are accomplished and have a better idea of what I have to accomplish to be successful. I know that requires a team effort."

Your team is everything at this point in your career, and strategy is paramount.

STRATEGIZING AND THE "ROLODEX COMPARISON"
What about your team approach on the road to success?

Los Angeles entertainment attorney Henry Root speaks about the all-important "Rolodex comparison" when discussing the benefit of frequent strategizing with the other members of the artist's team. As Henry explains, "It is an analysis and understanding of 'who knows who' and 'who can get to who,' in order to advance the artist's career agenda. As the artist gains national, if not international prominence, the issue of 'who can get to who' discussed among the team members becomes increasingly important."

And how close are the players in the entertainment industry? Henry states, "We're all aware of the concept of six degrees of separation, but in the very small world of the entertainment industry, it's more often one degree of separation. If I need to get to you and I don't know you, it's generally not more than one phone call or email for me to find someone who does know you and is willing to make an introduction for me."

Los Angeles entertainment attorney Susan Schaefer comments on strategizing, observing, "It is important at all stages of a client's career. And changing strategy is also important when the client's career changes."

Similarly, your focus on your work must continue unabated and you should work in conjunction with your team by pursuing your leads as you refine your work and build your reputation. In this respect, remember that you are conducting business with a group of dedicated professionals who have your best interests in mind. This is your opportunity to learn from them and build upon their expertise in order to advance your career.

INSTANT REPLAY

Your team is now in place and, as a unit, should chart your course for success in a unified fashion. Strategize with your team, understanding the working role of each team member and learning from all of them so that you may enhance your chances for success.

AND IT'S A WRAP

And it's a wrap, with some thoughts for your consideration.

The members of your team can play a critically important role in the development of your career as an artist within the entertainment industry. Your entertainment attorney will act as a counselor and advisor as well as a facilitator on your behalf, guiding you through the maze of legal and business issues with which you will be confronted during your career.

Your talent manager will work closely with your attorney and will provide career guidance, assisting you in exploiting your talents for the entertainment industry. Your literary manager and writing coach will provide you with literary direction and editorial assistance at appropriate times.

Your agent will present you with the proper guidance and industry connections to enhance opportunities in your career. Your editor will assist you in the professional editing of any content that may accompany your work and will work closely with your literary manager and writing coach.

Your producer will help you present your work to the world while defining your style and brand within the industry, ensuring that you are remaining on your chosen artistic path. And your publicist will define your image, public persona, and reputation in the industry.

When strategizing with your team and organizing conferences and meetings, always maintain a constant dialogue with the team members so that you will better understand your career path and make the right decisions in moving forward toward success in the entertainment industry.

FILM

* Your team will be indispensible in the motion picture industry, where productions can be complicated and lengthy, and where pre-production, production, and post-production problems often require immediate and sophisticated solutions, particularly in the independent film market.
* The caveat here is to expect and anticipate legal and business issues on an artistic and commercial level within the industry. That is the purpose of having your team in place.

TELEVISION

★ The television industry is still primarily based upon the airing of programming on the national networks. In this regard, your team will be able to focus its energies on the significance of network-placed content.

★ This permits a narrower focus on issues that may arise. Needless to say, the entire team will be involved in your work and will hopefully contribute to your success in television.

MUSIC

★ Team effort is very important in the music industry, where a myriad of opportunities exist for the rising star as well as the star soon to be on the rise.

★ The growing market for independent artists requires that your team be prepared and ready to assist at a moment's notice.

THE LITERARY ARTS

★ Like the music industry, the publishing industry has taken an independent turn. Of course, writers still rule in the world of the written word.

★ Your team will be essential to your success, from the inception of an idea for a book to its creation and publication. In this genre, everyone on the team will be involved in helping you find success.

FASHION AND MODELING

★ Designers and models who work in these industries rely very heavily on their team members to ensure success, especially regarding the presentation of their fashions and the models who showcase them.

★ Your team must be ready to assist in making the magic happen on the runways of the major fashion shows around the world.

THE VISUAL ARTS AND THE FINE ARTS

★ Typically, your team in the visual arts will move quickly in dealing with the issues of the day, which will often have to do with the placing of artwork or photography in museums or galleries.

★ The development of digital content is redefining the industry, and your team, and particularly your attorney, will be important in dealing with such issues.

TEAM HUDDLE

Your entire team will have respect and understanding for your gifts and talents as an artist and will provide you with the professional assistance you will need as you take your path to success in the new entertainment industry. Welcome to the place where creativity and imagination reign. Your team is with you!

Your attorney can become the facilitator for the presentation of your works within the industry. Just as your work must be creative and dynamic, your lawyer will be equally creative and dynamic in devising an approach to assist you in understanding the legal and business aspects of your career.

- ★ Your talent manager will recognize which of your particular gifts as an artist may be most important to your career.
- ★ Your literary manager and writing coach will help you formulate creative concepts and express yourself in writing.
- ★ Your agent will work closely with you to recognize which projects may bring the best business opportunities.
- ★ Your editor will personally collaborate with you on your projects in conjunction with your literary manager.
- ★ Your producer knows how to place your works in pre-production and production and bring them to life.
- ★ Your publicist will assist you in the public relations arena in presenting your talents to the world.

LIGHTS, CAMERA, ACTION!
Your team is in place. Now you are ready to be formally introduced to the entertainment industry.

A STORY INSPIRED BY A LEGENDARY MUSIC PRODUCER
He walked into the Weeks Recording Studio on the campus of the University of Miami with a smile and several jazz CDs in his hand.

I had spoken with him briefly on several occasions prior to our engineering and mixing session, but this was the first opportunity that I had time to speak to him in depth. I was fortunate to be referred to this producer by music industry colleagues, who informed me that he was a genius in the studio.

A native New Yorker, he was part of the founding team at Atlantic Records and directly involved in producing the incredible array of talent that walked through the doors of that label. When he relocated to South Florida, everyone referred to the studio where he engineered as "Atlantic Records South."

He was a prolific producer, and he had worked with such internationally known pop and rock artists as Aretha Franklin, Rod Stewart, the Allman Brothers, Eric Clapton, the Bee Gees, and many others. Honored and revered in the world of music, the Recording Academy presented the coveted Trustees Award to him for his significant contributions to the recording industry.

We sat and spoke about music.

I asked him to listen to a project originally produced at Track Studios in Washington, DC, titled *Sail into the Sun*. The recording had initially received airplay in the Northeast, but the production could be greatly improved for a re-release.

I introduced him to the assistant engineer on duty and instructed the engineer to play the current track. The producer first stood and listened, began to tap his foot, then slowly walked over to the console and sat as he continued to listen.

After he heard the song, he turned to me and said he would like to remix it, telling me it was excellent.

"Who wrote it?" he asked.

"I did," I replied.

"Nice job," he commented. "And who sang it?"

I hesitated and answered, "I did."

He smiled. "Impressive. I like how you wrap your vocals around the lyrics. It reminds me a little of Barry Gibb. Let's go to work on it!"

With that exchange, he proceeded to remix and re-engineer the song. I sat next to the console and watched him work his magic, patiently listening to each track and delicately moving the controls until he had found the right mix.

Four days later, he completed the mix and handed it to me. When I played it, the music seemed to jump off the CD, revealing a beautifully produced work.

Sail into the Sun was later released and promoted nationally, reaching the Top 20 on the Friday Morning Quarterback (FMQB) national adult-contemporary charts and performed in the motion picture and docu-concert, *Concert.*

And it was all because of the engineer and producer who brought the song back to life.

He was a man of great talent, gifted in his music expertise, who touched everyone who had the good fortune to work with him.

He was one of the greatest producers in the history of American pop, rock, and R&B music.

He was the late, legendary Tom Dowd.

And he was an artist.

FOUR

YOUR PROFESSIONAL ARTISTIC INTRODUCTION TO THE INDUSTRY

The road's a long and lonely place, it seems to me
Of one night stands and barroom bands
And midnight melodies
Well, I promise you it won't be long and
I'm just here to sing my song and
Thinking 'bout you back in Tennessee.

Richard Warren Rappaport, "Country Cowboy,"
from the motion picture soundtrack of *Concert*

THE BASICS

This chapter is about your professional introduction to the entertainment industry as you coordinate with your team for the road ahead. The choice of a proper legal entity for the development of your career is discussed, including the limitations of personal liability and the tax implications of your chosen legal entity.

An overview of the presentation process is also addressed, along with the tailoring of a strategy by your team to fit your professional needs and reach your goals while you continue to maintain a clear focus on your work. Your team's approach to implementing this strategy is discussed; you and your team will make the presentation, or "pitch," and hope to avoid the "pass" in order to get to the "green light" that will move you further along the road to success.

Lastly, the particular expertise of each of your team members is analyzed as they assist you in developing your reputation and credentials within the industry.

WHY THIS CHAPTER IS IMPORTANT TO YOU

You will soon be formally introduced to the industry. The entertainment industry, in particular, observes protocol when such introductions are made. This chapter is about that protocol.

FILM

* The importance of receiving the proper introduction as a producer, director, screenwriter, or actor should not be underestimated. It can be critical to your success. That introduction is typically made by your entertainment attorney or another representative from your team.

* Once the introduction is made, you will be involved in the business side of the industry. There will be other introductions, of course, and you will begin to develop your name and reputation in the world of film.

TELEVISION

* As in film, the television industry is always receptive to

individuals who are talented and wish to present their works for development.

★ Protocol is everything in television, where introductions are generally personal and made through your team. This will open the doors to established industry contacts.

MUSIC

★ Though the music industry offers the opportunity for individuals to perform and be "discovered," the importance of professional introductions to prominent music producers, publishers, and record labels can be critical to your success.

★ Your team will play a pivotal role in opening those doors.

THE LITERARY ARTS

★ Attorneys, agents, literary managers, and other members of your team will work closely together in order to find a publisher for your book. This will require introductions within the publishing industry.

★ Publishers expect to deal with your team and will welcome introductions by them.

FASHION AND MODELING

★ The fashion and modeling industries live on personal introductions. Your team will play an integral part in making them.

★ The introductions you make early in your career in these industries may be critical to your success.

THE VISUAL ARTS AND THE FINE ARTS

★ The world of the visual arts and fine arts is composed of a tightly knit group of individuals; introductions are crucial.

★ Here, opportunities may arise when you least expect them. And that happens when you are introduced to the right people.

It is time for your introduction to the entertainment industry.

— THE COURT OF ARTISTIC OPINION —
"COUNSELORS, APPROACH THE BENCH"

Now you are ready and prepared as you open the doors of the Court of Artistic Opinion and enter the courtroom.

Next to you is your entertainment attorney. Behind your attorney is your talent manager, literary manager, agent, editor, producer, and publicist. You walk past the spectators and sit with your attorney at a table in front of the judge's bench. To your right is another table where the opposing attorney sits; this attorney represents the entertainment industry.

Your attorney and opposing counsel shake hands. The bailiff announces the judge's entrance and the entire courtroom stands. The judge represents all that is fair and equitable in the arts and public opinion regarding the quality and artistic and commercial viability of your works.

Court is now in session. The judge addresses the attorneys. "Counselors, approach the bench."

Your attorney will speak on your behalf in discussing the worth and value of your work. Opposing counsel will discuss the industry's position and its initial impression of your work. The judge will be the arbiter of the facts, providing a glimpse of the public's opinion of your artistry.

You are now in the big leagues, where careers can begin and stars are born. And this is just the beginning.

YOUR PROFESSIONAL INTRODUCTION AND PRESENTATION WITHIN THE INDUSTRY

You have come to the point where you are ready to conquer the world of entertainment. You know that somewhere out there, the Hollywood Walk of Fame is waiting, and there is a star reserved for you. And your team is behind you and ready to begin.

In addition to your talent, it may very well be the team effort that will define your success or failure in the entertainment industry. In this regard, you should all operate in unison, with a clear focus on the work ahead.

The great benefit of having your team formally present you within the industry, regardless of where and how the presentation takes place, is that you will have the advice and assistance of experienced professionals by your side as you chart your path.

CHOOSING YOUR LEGAL ENTITY

To conduct business within the entertainment industry, one of the matters your attorney will discuss is the choice of a legal entity, which you will need, regardless of the entertainment genre in which you work. Your entertainment attorney will either have this discussion with you or will recommend an attorney versed in corporate law.

Boca Raton corporate attorney Gregory St. John III states that when considering the choice of a legal entity, there are three types of entities from which to choose: a sole proprietorship, a corporation, or a limited liability company. Greg discusses two important aspects to consider when making that choice: (1) tax implications of the legal entity and (2) limitations of personal liability. Both are explained below.

TAX IMPLICATIONS OF THE LEGAL ENTITY

Greg explains, "If the artist has not created a legal entity, he or she is considered to be a sole proprietorship, and all income and expenses are reported on the artist's individual tax return on a Schedule C. Most things that are deductible can be deducted in a corporate tax return or a Schedule C. However, there are some obscure benefits for health care insurance and pensions that favor incorporation."

And what of deductions in business?

Greg comments, "There is also a feeling that things can be deducted more easily on a corporate return than on a Schedule C, but that probably comes from the fact that individuals are more likely to be audited than entities. Generally, the only thing that matters is whether an expense is deductible as a business expense or not. Likewise, whether or not an artist is incorporated will not reduce the amount of income that is reportable in the tax return."

Greg also states that some tax professionals claim that being incorporated will save on taxes. However, the savings very often don't even pay for the cost of preparing the corporate tax return. He feels that the only way to know for sure is to prepare a pro forma return both ways using real numbers, such as last year's income and expenses.

Greg remarks that if the artist's attorney determines that a corporation is best, the artist may be able to elect to have the corporation treated like a small business corporation or Subchapter S (Sub-S) corporation, which is regarded as a pass-through entity. "What this essentially means is that the artist's income and expenses will be computed at the corporate level, but no tax is assessed at that level. Instead, the net income or net loss is passed through to the corporate shareholders, according to their percentage of ownership. For example, if a Sub-S corporation with two equal shareholders had $100,000 of income and $80,000 of expenses, each shareholder would get a K-1 form that showed $10,000 of income each."

However, Greg notes that the major limitations of the Sub-S corporation are that it can only have one class of stock and no preferential stock, that all of its shareholders must be natural persons (except for certain trusts) who are U.S. residents, and that it can have no more than 100 shareholders.

LIMITATIONS OF PERSONAL LIABILITY

On the critical matter of limitation of personal liability, Greg remarks, "As people, we are all responsible for our actions. However, doing business through a corporation or limited liability company may offer some protection from certain types of claims, but not necessarily all claims. For example, if there is a concert equipment rental bill for equipment that was rented in the name of the business entity, then the principals will generally not be responsible. However, if the sole owner of a business is also the only employee, and if he or she assaults another person in a fight, then both the person and the business might be responsible."

Thus, in order to maximize the limitation of liability, Greg stresses that the business must be properly set up, requiring that it file annual reports with the state of organization and maintain separate business cards, telephone numbers, and the like. "You can't mix your personal life with the business's life. For example, it's important to have separate bank accounts. You can't comingle personal funds with business money. And when signing business papers, always include your title, e.g., John Doe, President. This is a complicated topic, but in general, if you don't respect the business entity as a separate being, don't expect the court to respect it."

Greg discusses the fact that the limited liability company, or LLC, has come into favor as a legal entity. "It enjoys the same pass-through entity status as a Sub-S corporation, and it doesn't have any of the limitations to qualify. So, if you wanted to have another business as an equity owner, an LLC would be better than a corporation. However, an LLC requires operating agreements, which can be quite detailed and complicated, depending on the needs of the parties. Of course, such documents can be created by your attorney."

Finally, Greg provides insight on the artist's choice to do business under a Sub-S corporation or LLC. "Remember that each year you must file an annual report with the state of incorporation or organization, and if you fail to do so your entity may be administratively dissolved. You must also file a separate income tax return for your entity. There may be other costs or expenses, such as city taxes, depending on where you live. Most states respect the federal income tax treatment. Sub-S and LLC entities are generally not taxed on their income at the state level. However, some states do impose income taxes. Check with a tax professional in your state."

Basically, any decision with respect to the creation of a legal entity must be made based on the advice of your attorney or another attorney whose practice is in the area of corporate law. But once you have established the entity, your path to success will be that much more secure.

INSTANT REPLAY

Now that your team is in place and you are ready to conquer the industry and the world, your attorney will deal with the question of the type of legal entity to utilize. During your discussions with your attorney, you will learn about the tax implications of such a legal entity and the importance of that entity in reducing personal liability.

THE PRESENTATION PROCESS

Whether you are pursuing opportunities within a major company—such as a film studio, record label, television network, publishing company, nationally known art gallery, or dance company—or planning to build your own company in order to showcase your talents, you must continue to coordinate with your entire team in the presentation process in order to ensure the greatest chance for success.

You will be formally introduced to established industry professionals who may have the ability to help you and to launch your career. This is generally accomplished through your entertainment attorney, manager, or agent with the assistance of the other members of your team. Your presentation within the industry will be essential in seeking that sometimes elusive but rewarding development deal that can launch your career.

For example, if you are making a presentation of a screenplay to a film or television studio, the presentation or pitch will, in all likelihood, be made by your representative, such as your lawyer, literary manager, agent, or some combination thereof. Or if you are planning a showcase concert at a famous music venue, your personal talent manager will most likely plan that in conjunction with a booking agent.

Regardless of the particular plan for presentation of your art, it must be accomplished with full and complete coordination among the members of your team, taking into account the clear vision of your goal, the preliminary timeline for achieving it, and the legal, business, and industry parameters for getting there.

TAILORING YOUR STRATEGY FOR THE PRESENTATION OR PITCH

How important is it for the artist to have his or her strategy tailored in the presentation?

From your position as the artist, your plan should be to think dynamically and be prepared to follow the advice of your team if the presentation must be revised during the presentation process. Thus, it is always best to analyze your work on a continuous basis, even while it is being presented. It is that sense of dedication to perfection and an understanding of the marketplace that can distinguish your work from others. In this regard, your goal should be to make every reasonable attempt to excel at your art and create the best presentation possible.

Entertainment attorney Henry Root states, "The needs of each artist, and the best way for each of them to achieve their individual goals, can vary dramatically from client to client. Regular strategic planning conversations with both the client and the other members of the client's team, including the client's personal manager, agent, and business manager, are essential elements of the 'counseling' part of being an attorney and counselor at law."

And entertainment attorney Emily Graham comments, "The project must be presented in both a business and artistic way. The business aspect must be clear and involve a concise and realistic business plan that is mindful of current economics, distribution, and marketing in the particular industry. The artistic aspect must deliver the message and be to the point."

Your team will assist you in fashioning your strategy as you move forward toward industry introductions. And remember that your strategy must be dynamic and subject to change if the situation warrants. So be flexible in the development of your career. That mindset will serve you well.

YOUR STRATEGIC DIRECTION FOR THE PRESENTATION

Direction is critically important. Ultimately, you want to orchestrate an entire career, and that is a noble thing to do. It should be your desire to constantly improve and refine your work, which will be critical to your success in the industry. And it all truly begins with you.

However, if there is one rule to which you should adhere, it is to prepare for the response that you or your team members may receive when making your presentation. There are hundreds or even thousands of projects being submitted for consideration in your area of the entertainment industry at any given time. However, you will find that whether your project is accepted or declined, those in the industry will begin to become aware of your presence. And that is an excellent start.

You and your team should expect one of two possibilities once the presentation or pitch is made: the "pass" or the "green light." The first discussion will be about the pass.

THE PASS

During the presentation, you must be prepared for all the typical bumps and bruises on your path to success. That includes the pass, or rejection of your work from an industry executive.

The rejection may have to do with the fact that the company to which you are presenting the project does not have the financial or other resources to commit to your project. Or the company does not work in the genre or style that applies to your work. Or perhaps the company has already committed to a project that is similar to yours. Or it is possible that the company simply passed for any number of other reasons having nothing to do with the quality of the project or your talents.

Such reasons are generally grounded in business and legal decisions that are separate and apart from the quality of your work. In fact, the quality of your work can, and often does, have nothing at all to do with it.

Just as an example, in the world of film, when pitching a story to a studio, producer and literary manager Ken Atchity comments that if a story is original, it's probably not for a major studio and is simply not a fit for that studio. This is primarily because of the nature of corporate ownership in the film industry today and the decision-making process within it, as well as the immense cost of films today, regardless of the quality of the project.

Ken states, "Studios in the last few years have gone to acquiring stories that have underlying property value, such as Broadway plays, high-visibility novels, and well-known comic books. The exception is a screenplay that has a major director and star firmly attached. All else, in today's filmmaking world, has become indie."

It is therefore very possible or even likely that you will receive several passes before your team approaches a company that finds you appealing as an artist and your project worthy of its attention and time. That is the green light that will take your career one more step forward.

DEALING WITH THE PASS AND LEARNING TO ACCEPT THE WORD *NO*

Celeste Jones, author and director of the Elementary Etiquette Society, comments on how an artist should be prepared to hear the word *no* when it applies to potential opportunities in his or her career, especially because today's *no* could become tomorrow's *yes*.

How should you conduct yourself under those circumstances? Celeste remarks, "As one door closes, another door opens. Never burn a bridge! An artist should set ego aside and be utterly gracious when being denied." Perhaps the most important thing to remember is that the industry is replete with stories of the most incredibly successful individuals who have had numerous passes on their works, until the right time and moment came for them and their work was accepted.

Thus, the endgame in the industry goes well beyond the quality, originality, and dynamic nature of your work. It has to do with your ability to withstand the rigors of what may be a delicate and lengthy presentation process and an understanding of protocol, or the rules of the road. In essence, it relates to your ability to convey to those in the industry with whom you may be working that you are a serious talent and a bright and articulate individual who is on the way to the top.

During this process, expect challenges and understand that such challenges are a part of the process on your path through the initial professional stages of your career.

> **INSTANT REPLAY**
> Strategy and focus are critical to enhancing your success within the entertainment industry as your attorney and the rest of your team engage in the presentation process.

MAINTAINING YOUR VISION AND FOCUS AFTER THE PASS

And what of maintaining your vision and focus during this interim period? How should you deal with this issue in order to enhance your chances for success?

Psychologist Dr. Andrea Corn feels the artist must be grounded enough to believe that he or she can make it. "An artist must be able to survive through the lean times, which means being supportive, patient, and accepting of oneself, even if it requires a second or third job to make ends meet. Sometimes accepting current circumstances is all an artist can do, even though his or her dream remains closely attached to the heart. Most importantly, one must remain humble and not blame others and accept responsibility for their own actions. All of those are part of maintaining a clear focus."

So once again, for you, the artist, it is vision and focus that count. Never forget that.

THE IMPORTANCE OF PATIENCE

As your team makes its presentations on your behalf, you must continue to be patient.

Author and college basketball coach Mike Jarvis also comments on the need for patience. "How important is patience? Probably as important as anything you do. Patience is one ingredient you will need to have more often than not, because when the project is new and unfolding as a creative piece, you cannot really control everything that is spinning around you as you work with your editor, literary manager, and attorney to finish it. Simply put, you are depending on a whole lot of other people."

Author Madeleine Kirsh found herself asking about patience in the process. "Patience? What is patience? I don't know. I work very hard and am used to results. Yes, it's hard to be patient. Yet it's necessary. Just look for forward momentum and results, but do not expect to get it unless you earn it."

Author Carolina Garcia-Aguilera tells us that patience is something you have to learn. And she also feels that you must also develop a thick skin and take nothing personally. "Please understand that in the publishing industry, it's all business, and patience is critical to your success. The rule is never to appear too pushy, or else you will seem desperate. And that makes it easier for them to give you a quick 'no' than a slow 'yes.'"

And editor Kate Burgauer states, "Patience is the name of the game in creative writing. In the writing stages, you must set aside time every day to write, rewrite, write, and rewrite again." Kate feels that written works are practically always in need of many stages of editing, and that you must view the project as a marathon and train accordingly. Kate also states that once the project is complete, the waiting still continues. "Since the world is flooded with creative products, you must understand that producers and publishers are the gatekeepers. There will be more rewrites, and there may even be a suggestion that another writer edit your work."

Patience is another name for the entertainment industry. Without it, nothing can happen. With it, careers can change for the better in an instant.

WAITING FOR THE GREEN LIGHT

If your talent warrants, you will find success during the presentation process as your team continues to work closely with you. In fact, the green light, or acceptance of your work for development, may be just around the corner. That will be discussed in the next chapter.

So in today's new entertainment industry, patience is not just a state of mind. It is a virtue and a journey. Please be patient and hopefully it will be a great ride.

Your team's expertise will be critical as you continue to present your works within the industry. Always remember to be patient in the process. It can be one of the best attributes you may develop.

INSTANT REPLAY

Remember to coordinate with your team during every step of the presentation process, understanding the nature of the presentations and the results of each pitch. Do not hesitate to work closely with your team members, who are there to assist you in your efforts. And maintain your focus at all times.

AND IT'S A WRAP

And it's a wrap, with some thoughts for your consideration.

Your team will begin the process of formally presenting you within the entertainment industry. During this period, you should coordinate and interact with your team members, utilizing the expertise that each member provides.

The road to success can be trying and difficult, but you must believe in yourself and your work, which will enhance the likelihood of success, as you maintain your vision and focus. Team coordination and patience will go a long way toward ensuring that your presentations are completely professional and will demonstrate to those in the industry that you are aware of the rules of the road and respect the process.

FILM

★ Whether you are an actor, director, producer, or screenwriter, your professional posture is critical within the motion picture industry. Hollywood is a fascinating town where everyone in the industry knows everyone else, and that makes it an interesting place to be, especially when opportunities can be within your reach.

★ Rely on the experience and wisdom of your team to make the proper introductions at the right time in order to begin walking the path to success.

TELEVISION

★ The television industry lives and breathes in New York and Los Angeles, and if this is your industry, you must be introduced to the right people to take you in the right direction for your career.

★ As with film, introductions are everything. Use the services and skills of your team. They mean everything.

MUSIC

★ The music industry is morphing at an ever-increasing rate as the digital world explodes, bringing new music and fresh talent to the world stage.

★ Your strategic plan should be to combine an understanding of your craft with a solid team and excellent connections and introductions. And that is just the beginning.

THE LITERARY ARTS

★ Writers are unique in that their skills permit them to spin a story and carry their readers with them.

★ Once you begin to establish yourself, use all of the connections that are available to you, particularly with respect to introductions within the film and television industries, which are places where great stories tend to be showcased.

THE VISUAL ARTS AND THE FINE ARTS

★ The visual arts and fine arts consist of a smaller and more compact group of individuals versed in their industries. Get to know them through your team, which can open doors for you.

★ Whether it is painting, photography, or the stage, the world can be yours if you are aware of how to use the connections you have been given through your team.

TEAM HUDDLE

Your team has begun to open the doors for your advancement in the industry. They are by your side as you move forward in your path toward success.

★ Your attorney will carefully guide you through the legal and business issues that arise during this introductory process, ensuring that your intellectual property and other proprietary rights are protected.

★ Your talent manager will understand the importance of reaching the right people for such introductions.

★ Your literary manager and writing coach will prepare you to express the nature of your work as an artist in your field.

★ Your agent will assist in facilitating industry introductions, always looking for opportunities on your behalf.

★ Your editor will continue to be available whenever needed and will coordinate with your literary manager if necessary.

★ Your producer can be critical in preparing the right visual content for your introductions.

★ Your publicist will help place that important spin on all you do as you are introduced to the industry.

LIGHTS, CAMERA, ACTION!

You've been introduced to the industry. Now you are ready for the next step. The world seems to stop turning as your attorney calls you with the incredible news that you are about to receive a contract. You have accomplished the seemingly impossible task of securing a development deal. It is truly a case of "Lights, Camera, Action!" That is coming in the next chapter.

A STORY INSPIRED BY A SCREENWRITER FROM NEW YORK CITY

It was something that she had wanted to write for years. She thought of a story about a beautiful, bright, and successful young woman in New York City who appears to have everything, except what she desires most: a normal father-daughter relationship with her dad, who is too preoccupied with his work to spend time with her.

And then our heroine meets the man of her dreams, although she will not realize that he is the one until it is almost too late.

This would be a story about love, forgiveness, and reconciliation.

And what was the genesis of this tale? Did the author live it, or at least parts of it?

In a sense, it was a part of her. It all began with a coffee cup that our writer held in her hand as she sat with her husband in front of a café in Manhattan on a beautiful spring evening. She knew she had a story to tell but struggled to arrange it in her head, thinking about how it might look on paper and whether it would be a book or screenplay.

To compound her troubles, she had no experience in writing either one. But she felt that the story had to be told.

And she was going to tell it.

The first thing she decided was that she would write a screenplay. She read everything she could about creative writing, storytelling, and story arcs, and studied the academic structure of the three act play. And after she carefully digested as much information as possible, she began to write, creating a step outline and treatment.

She was introduced to an entertainment attorney, an editor, and a literary manager, all of whom began to assist her, providing further direction. Now the story actually had a beginning, a middle, and an end. She continued to refine the outline drafts, one after another.

There were so many drafts that she lost count. But she still continued to write.

She noticed that the story was developing further. It was as if the characters, at first simply a jumble of names and relationships, began to slowly develop texture and to literally come alive. Each character became more complicated and difficult to predict, just as people in real life.

Once she finally completed a draft of the treatment, she began to write the screenplay, continuing to utilize the services of her editor, literary manager, and attorney to help guide her along the way. She was determined to finish the script and deliver a great story.

So she continued to piece it together, scene by scene, page by page, and act by act.

And each time she revised it, the story became more interesting, more complex, developing even more texture. Her characters had taken on a life of their own. She had brought her characters into the real world.

It was exciting!

And it all started as an idea over a cup of coffee at a café in New York City.

Her screenplay has the working title *Bing's Place*.

She is Robin Abramovitz Goldberg.

And she is an artist.

FIVE

YOUR BIG BREAK:
THE DEVELOPMENT DEAL

And then our lives, they turn 'round and around
Like a pinwheel that's blown by the breeze
Turning so fast that I know it can't last
And we'll never, never stop
Turning 'round and around.

Richard Warren Rappaport, "'Round and Around," from the
motion picture soundtrack of *Concert*

THE BASICS

This chapter is about the development deal in the entertainment industry, which can open the door to success in your career. The involvement of your team members in negotiating the deal is addressed, along with its collective approach to bringing that negotiation to a successful conclusion. In this regard, the deal is analyzed as one that should be in your best interests and contain a viable strategy for your success.

Your prospective business partners on the other side of the deal are discussed, including the reputation of such individuals and the quality of their organization. Your legal rights, responsibilities, and obligations under the deal are examined to be sure that all such rights are protected and that the agreement conforms to current industry standards and practices.

Other matters include the need to work with your team to determine an alternative strategy in the event that the development deal is terminated or collapses, as well as a plan in case the deal is resurrected, hopefully placing your career on track again. Moreover, the vital importance of protecting your intellectual property rights will be considered, as well as the relevance and significance of potential litigation in protecting those rights under the law.

Lastly, this chapter discusses alternative dispute resolution and its importance in resolving contractual disputes, in order to avoid the expense of litigation as your career continues to move forward.

WHY THIS CHAPTER IS IMPORTANT TO YOU

Your development deal can be the start of your professional career and the beginning of your ascent within the industry.

FILM

* Development deals in the film industry will generally relate to projects that are placed in development by independent producers, literary managers, the mini-major studios, or the major studios.

* Regardless of how they are initiated, they can mark the beginning of a new or expanding career for the screen-

writer, producer, director, actor, or anyone in front of or behind the camera.

TELEVISION

★ Development deals in the television industry follow a similar structure and path to those found in film. Once a television network or production company decides to develop a project, it is earmarked for development and broadcast.

★ Typically, such deals move quickly from development into principal photography, completion, and distribution.

MUSIC

★ Development deals have historically involved artists signed to major label record deals but now can pertain to all artists, because many create their own companies and deals in this new digital age of independent labels.

★ Regardless of the type of deal, the artist will work with the label to produce a CD, structure a strategic marketing plan, and set up a regional or national tour in order to find success in the music industry.

THE LITERARY ARTS

★ Once an author signs with a major publisher in a development deal, the book, when complete, will be placed in distribution and promoted by the publishing company.

★ Development deals in publishing are unique in that writers will tend to slowly build an audience of loyal readers. And as long as a writer never stops writing, his or her career can last a lifetime.

FASHION AND MODELING

★ In fashion, deals or agreements to develop the styles of a designer can vary widely, depending on whether a designer joins a larger company or starts his or her own company and looks for distribution.

★ Models are not involved in traditional development deals as they are referenced in other areas of the entertainment industry, unless they are working in another genre, such as acting for film or television. More typically, a model may sign with an agency that will promote him or her in the media, which is a form of development and branding.

THE VISUAL ARTS AND THE FINE ARTS

★ Visual artists will often sign agreements with galleries, through their agents, for short-term exhibits. This type of deal is basically utilized to present an artist and his or her works within the industry.

★ Regardless, the development of a visual artist's career is generally predicated on long-term exposure through galleries around the country and abroad.

— THE COURT OF ARTISTIC OPINION —
"COUNSELORS, APPROACH THE BENCH"

Once again, you are back before the Court of Artistic Opinion. Your counselor surveys the courtroom, looks at the judge and opposing counsel, glances at you, smiles, and whispers, "We're going to win!"

The development deal will require the assistance and guidance of your entertainment attorney, who will be well-versed in creating, reviewing, and negotiating such an agreement.

With the advice and consent of your other team members, you can be assured that any such deal will be subject to the proper scrutiny and will provide you with knowledge so that you may take advantage of the opportunities that will let you reach the goals you have worked so hard to attain.

Regardless of the genre in which you are involved, the development of your career is critical, and this chapter is what that is all about.

THE DEVELOPMENT DEAL

The development deal in the entertainment industry may very well be the watershed of your ascent toward success in your artistry. This deal is a contract or agreement offered by an individual, company, or entity that has an interest in professionally developing your career and presenting you artistically and commercially within the entertainment industry.

These deals are generally brought to you by a member of your team, such as the attorney, talent manager, literary manager, or agent, following the presentation or pitch and a favorable response from the entity to which it was presented.

Entertainment attorney and author Todd Brabec comments on the nature of such deals. "Development deals in today's world are essential, as they are designed to take one's skills and career to a new level and hopefully a wider audience. One can improve his or her craft through these deals as well as gain a greater sense of professionalism, both of which are necessary if one wants to succeed in entertainment."

The one constant is that the development deal will vary in each situation and be based on the particular parameters evident for that particular deal. And each development deal stands or falls on its own, requiring different contractual and artistic approaches in order to maximize the likelihood of success.

Obviously, the protocol to be followed is for your team to evaluate the deal and explain it to you in layman's terms, in a way that makes clear not only what is within the "four corners" of the agreement, but, equally important, to understand what is outside those four corners; namely, the reputation within the industry of the company or individual that proposes to work with you.

UNDERSTANDING THE DEAL

How important is it to understand the deal?

Entertainment attorney Henry Root speaks of the need to examine all development deals very carefully in today's business climate, to be certain the deal is in the best interests of the artist. He states, "Take a new and developing recording artist being offered a first exclusive recording agreement as an example. At our firm, there is no 'off the rack' deal, even if we are negotiating with a recording company with which we have previously done contracts for other clients. At each step of the negotiations, we strategize with the client, their personal manager, and others on their team, if necessary, as to what terms are essential to further the client's career."

And how case specific is such strategizing?

Henry comments, "We may bring in the client's business manager to review the accounting provisions. A pop artist might need to obtain a commitment to produce a video or a radio promotion commitment, whereas a rock artist might need a financial guarantee for tour support. On the other hand, a solo artist might need a guaranteed budget to assemble and rehearse a touring backing band once the record is delivered, where a group artist might need a budget from which to purchase equipment, musical instruments, and other tour gear before they hit the road."

Entertainment attorney Joseph Serling also discusses the particular elements of a development deal in the music industry. "The most important thing in development deals is to ensure that the length of the deal is as short as possible. Furthermore, the attorney needs to make sure that the development deal, in addition to providing for the payment of recording costs, has a mechanism for the ownership of the masters to revert back to the artist, unless it's a license deal, in the event the deal does not move forward to a full-blown record contract. Additionally, the royalties payable to the artist, both record and mechanicals, are very important."

Joe talks of the approach to take in representing his music clients in indie-styled deals. "I ask what sort of financial resources are available to fund the venture and what are the short- and long-term goals of the private indie label? Is this label for one artist or numerous artists? What are the genres of music? Is there a desire to sell or assign the artist to a major label? What are the distribution choices? Are they for a major label, indie label, or self-distribution, and is distribution both physical and digital? What are the marketing and promotion plans for each artist? And I also ask if there is a constant evaluation of the project from a marketing and promotion standpoint, and an evaluation from a business perspective."

Entertainment attorney Dixon Dern remarks on development deals in film and television. "Basically, if it is development of a property for a movie or television project, I check into the worthiness of the party who has approached them. Is this a reputable producer or distributor? Then I evaluate with the client the terms of the proposed development deal. To me, the major factors are my client's role in development and production, the money, the credit, and the ownership or back-end participation position. If my client is a member of the Writers Guild of America (WGA), I make sure that the deal for his writing services is clearly covered under the WGA agreement. The same would be true of a director through the Directors Guild of America."

As can be seen from the comments above, the structure and content of a development deal will vary, depending on such factors as its application within a particular segment of the entertainment industry, the type of artistic involvement that is the subject of the deal, the company presenting the deal, and the business environment in which it is offered.

OWNERSHIP AND PROTECTION OF YOUR INTELLECTUAL PROPERTY IN THE DEAL

Your attorney should ensure that your intellectual property is protected during the course of negotiations in a development deal.

Entertainment attorney Kim Kolback recommends that her clients always try to retain ownership of their intellectual property. This permits them to license, transfer, or assign short-term or limited rights to multiple parties, which results in more control over the use of the material and potential financial gain.

New York and Ann Arbor entertainment and sports attorney Gregory L. Curtner adds that intellectual property should be carefully documented and appropriate registrations should be professionally filed and maintained. And Dixon Dern also stresses the importance of protecting your intellectual property rights, stating, "If intellectual property is copyrightable, then clearly, I would have the property copyrighted. Also, if there are any trademark aspects to a property, such as a trade name, I will encourage the client to get federal trademark protection."

Dixon speaks of instances where clients must submit their intellectual property to studios in the form of treatments and screenplays. "There is usually a requirement by the studio that the submitting party sign a release form, releasing the studio if it uses a similar property. Thus, whenever a client makes a submission, I encourage them to cover it with a letter to prove that they in fact did submit it, in case a similarity claim does arise. In Hollywood, most studios now require the submission through an agent or attorney, thinking that that act may protect them from similarity suits. It probably does not, but it's a try in that direction."

Todd Brabec talks about the importance of intellectual property rights in the entertainment industry, stating, "The attorney must make his or her clients aware of their rights and what they really mean, both in a business and legal sense as well as a financial sense. Registration requirements must always be met, and monitoring uses of one's work is essential." Todd believes that a good and open relationship with those entrusted with administering one's rights is a necessity. "The best thing an attorney can do is to explain fully the ramifications of any deal being made for the exploitation of rights."

Entertainment attorney George Stein discusses the protection of intellectual property rights, claiming it is of fundamental importance. "The client should understand the importance of copyright protection and registration, and should also be aware of the ramifications of work-made-for-hire situations, when the intellectual property will be owned by another person or entity. The attorney should stress the necessity of attorney-generated written agreements between parties when issues exist such as creation and authorship, payment, percentage splits, creative control, and administration and control of rights, as in sales and licensing."

And entertainment attorney Joseph Arrington states, "I advise my clients to protect their intellectual property rights at all costs. These rights are the true assets that will provide them income, and preserving these rights properly is their true business. The exploitation and commercialization of these rights are just a natural extension of their career."

Obviously, protecting your intellectual property rights may be one of the most critical and important aspects of your career in the arts. You, the artist, must remember that there may be no greater value than the ownership and protection of your intellectual property interests during your career. Protect your works. They belong to you.

INSTANT REPLAY

Your intellectual property may be the most valuable asset you may own as an artist. Protect it! Your attorney and the rest of your team will be the guardians of your intellectual property, which can define the level of success attained in your career.

THE TEAM APPROACH IN THE DEAL

How significant is your team and its approach to the development deal?

Talent manager Wayne Baxley speaks of development deals and the importance of your team in evaluating them. "The team is always important in terms of how you run your overall business. Most of the time, the artist is only as good as the team or the people around that artist, handling the everyday things that allow him or her to perform to their highest capabilities."

However, Wayne adds a caveat, claiming that it is critical to have clarification on the roles of the various team members in order for the artist to progress in this business. He also underscores the need for the team to believe in the artist and be efficient and productive in order to properly represent the artist.

Wayne states, "Our team consists solely of Sommore and me, and I handle the management, bookings, and just about everything that pertains to the business of Sommore. However, based on the different situations that we face in this ever-changing business environment, we do have our attorneys, accountants, and other professionals that we consult with on a regular basis, as well as our stylists, make-up artists, and publicist to assist with Sommore's overall public perception. Together, each and every person on our team does their part to contribute to the success of Sommore."

Henry Root has discussed development deals with his clients in practically all genres of the industry and has opinions about how to prepare the artist for the possibility that the deal may require substantial negotiating in order for it to be acceptable and remain in accordance with current industry standards and practices. "The main problem with development deals is that typically the artist has zero leverage, often combined with unrealistic expectations of the material terms that the artist feels he or she is entitled to receive. And sometimes the development offers are just plain silly."

Henry gives an interesting example of such a deal. "I recently received a development offer for a television series for my client where the only obligations of the offering producer were to obtain an 'expression of interest' (defined as 'no less than a commitment to schedule a pitch meeting') for the financing, production, and broadcast of the series from a national television exhibition entity, and if such an 'expression of interest' was secured within the initial six months, the 'development term' would be automatically extended for an additional six months, within which the producer was to attempt to secure 'no less than a verbal production order' from a national television exhibition entity."

Producer and literary manager Ken Atchity adds, "To me, the only approach in today's world of volatile change is thinking outside the box, entrepreneurially. So I'd be careful to agree with any 'rules' when it comes to Hollywood or publishing these days."

Perhaps you can begin to see why the development deal calls for a thorough discussion between the artist and his or her attorney and other members of the team. All such deals must be very carefully analyzed and discussed prior to any decision to move forward with them.

And though the financial cost is always an issue, especially when you are at the start of your career, that cost may be well worth it. Producer and broadcaster René Katz comments, "Always remember that while there is a financial cost to utilizing the professional services of your team, the expense you incur is well worth the expertise you gain. In the other direction, the knowledge you obtain permits you to reduce your mistakes to their irreducible minimum. So if one deal falls through, another one will soon be on the way."

Basically, the professional and experienced approach of your team will be very important in evaluating the development deal and your chances for success in the entertainment industry.

INSTANT REPLAY

The development deal may define the scope and direction of your career as an artist. It is important that your attorney and your team negotiate a deal that is in your best interests and that presents a strategy for the further development of your career.

YOUR PARTNERS ON THE OTHER SIDE OF THE DEAL

One vital element of the development deal that will exist outside the four corners of the written agreement has to do with the people and company with which you will be in business once the deal is executed.

Joseph Arrington speaks of one critical point in evaluating these deals. "My biggest concern with development deals is ensuring that the parties who seek to partner with the client are really legitimate partners and are providing the client an exit strategy in the event the partnership doesn't meet expectations."

In the evaluation of a development deal, entertainment attorney Emily Graham comments, "Regardless of the genre, what you should look for will be the quality of the company and of the people who present the deal. Experience in the industry is essential as well as a track record of past success."

And how important are these factors?

Emily suggests, "They may not be the most determinative factors on the quality and worth of a project. However, as part of the whole picture, they can be very important as to whether the project will eventually get 'picked up.' In evaluating a project for indies and people who are relatively new to the industry, I would look for factors such as realistic expectations in evaluating a project, honesty, business integrity and savvy, monetization of the project, and the acceptance of risk."

Kim Kolback provides insight as to how she represents the emerging artist in a development deal. "When new talent arrives at the steps of my office, it is usually in the negotiation stages of a deal. I sit with the client to determine what the parties discussed and agreed upon. I then explain the process for negotiating the deal. Because the new artist is generally the 'hungrier' party, I advise the client that he or she needs to be prepared to compromise in order to make the deal happen."

Ultimately, it all comes down to the language in the agreement. And your experienced attorney is skilled in dealing with that.

REVIEWING THE AGREEMENT

Kim discusses the next steps in the process. "Presuming the other party sends over the initial draft of an agreement, which is generally the case, I will review it on behalf of my client and make all of the desired changes he or she would like in that agreement." Kim will then schedule a meeting and educate the client by carefully reviewing and explaining the terms of the agreement and all the changes being sought.

She will also warn the client that it is unlikely that he or she will get all of the proposed changes. "I will ask the client to identify what are believed to be the ten or so most important changes in the contract. Of course, money is always significant to the client and I try to explain that the duration of an agreement and retention of intellectual property rights are also critical terms upon which the client should stand firm."

Based upon her conversations with the client, Kim will negotiate for as much as she can, always pushing for as many concessions as possible.

As an alternative, Kim recommends that her client submit the initial draft of any agreement for negotiations. Though this will cost more in legal fees because of the time needed to prepare that agreement, it will provide the most favorable terms for the client from the outset. Thus, the client generally ends up with better overall terms in the final agreement.

Television personality and spokesperson Jenna Edwards has an interesting and far-sighted perspective when she speaks of the individuals on the other side of the deal. "Because I am so closely aligned with a nonprofit organization, I always look at the repercussions on the organization's reputation. If I were a donor, what would I think about a charity that is run by the same person that represents that product? Even if it's not a direct alignment, I will only associate my name and image with products and companies that can support the credibility of the nonprofit organization. On that same note, I am also more willing to negotiate on rates if the client can offer support to the charity, which is my other major pursuit."

Thus, always try to be involved in negotiations and strategizing when discussing your future business partners in any development deal, and be prepared to provide input when your attorney or other member of your team requests it. And if you do not understand the nature of a particular strategy, ask your attorney to explain it to you, so that you are constantly in the loop in these negotiations.

INSTANT REPLAY

When considering a development deal, it is important to look outside the four corners of the agreement by qualifying your potential new business partners. Your attorney should review the terms of the development deal on a point-by-point basis. If necessary, other members of your team may be called in to discuss it as well.

THE DEAL AND YOUR CAREER

Your attorney will invariably cover the business and legal aspects of the agreement, including a discussion of issues relating to potential or prospective liability under that agreement. A concurrent issue is whether your prospective partners are litigious in the handling of disputes.

All these elements and others, known as "deal points," will of course have to be reviewed by your team, and particularly your entertainment attorney, to be certain that the deal conforms with the law and to current industry standards and practices within that aspect of the industry.

The deal points can include elements that may define your career ahead. Your attorney should provide a proper explanation so that you are thoroughly informed and understand the deal.

PROTECTING YOUR RIGHTS UNDER THE DEAL

Specifically, your attorney will review the deal in order to be assured that your rights are protected under the contact and in accordance with state and federal law.

He or she will also look for important clauses that pertain to such things as how you will be paid upon execution of the agreement, whether that payment will represent an advance against royalties or a nonrefundable payment, and whether there are sufficient safeguards in the event of a dispute, such as enough time for you to cure a breach alleged by the other party and other elements.

Entertainment attorney Susan Schaefer comments on such deals. "These deals depend on whether the client is a writer, director, actor, or composer, or performs another function. But in general, the important terms to cover are whether or not the project will move the client's career forward, or whether the client wants to do the project for another reason."

Susan states that the deal may depend upon other factors. "I look at whether the production company has a good track record or reputation for getting projects made and what are the main billing/credit and financial terms (including whether there will be any split of profits or any residuals paid to the client in addition to upfront money), the length of time the client will be tied up with the project during development, and whether or not the client will be required to devote his or her services exclusively to the project for any length of time."

What of the artist's expectations during this period of negotiations?

Henry Root speaks to this issue. "The notion of preparing the client for the fact that the deal may need substantial negotiations in order for it to be acceptable is not always easy. Managing the client's expectations is important so that they will conform to the reality of the results that can be obtained, taking into account the complexity of the deal, the degree of leverage or lack thereof under the circumstances, and the amount of the fees or percentage fees under which the negotiations will be undertaken by counsel."

WHEN THE DEAL GOES SOUTH

Most of the time, the entity presenting you with the deal, whether it is a film studio, television network, record label, or any other company, will have an "exit" clause, which will permit them to terminate the agreement in certain circumstances.

These circumstances may have nothing at all to do with your artistic talents or the merits of your project. The reasons may be based on the condition of the company that signed you on with your project, the economy, the nature of the industry at that time and significant changes within it, or any other reason unrelated to you directly but still impacting you or your project.

Once your deal is terminated, it is important to remember that if the project is good, the likelihood is strong that you will be offered other deals and opportunities, hopefully soon. In fact, there may be other entities that could regard the availability of your project within the industry as a tremendous opportunity, and they may be interested in approaching you.

Furthermore, in evaluating and analyzing why the deal was terminated, you and your team should study it as an intellectual model to determine what needs to be done to carry you forward in the industry. Your attorney will be best able to review the situation and will also seek the advice of your manager and agent for an industry-based view of the significance of what occurred.

ADVICE FROM YOUR TEAM

Regardless of the outcome, it is important to look to your team for solid advice, remembering that each of these professionals possesses skills beyond your own and, though there may be differing opinions on the direction of your career, they should be dedicated to your success. Your lack of understanding is only a negative in this industry, so do not hesitate to ask questions of your team at any time.

In essence, it's good logic to maintain your emotional balance and a positive demeanor while "in between jobs," as you wait for your team to bring you the next development deal. By keeping your head up and letting the world know that you are resilient in handling the expected ups and downs of your career, you will become known within the industry as someone to call for work.

WHEN THE DEAL COMES NORTH AGAIN: THE NEW DEAL

With hard work, good planning, and just a little bit of luck, you will find that other deals will come your way. As in the past, when that occurs, you should seek the advice of your team, in order to evaluate the deal and make decisions as to its worth.

In other words, the entire cycle repeats itself as your team comes together to help you conquer the world with your new deal. So when the telephone rings at the office of your attorney, manager, or agent, and you are informed that a new deal has been offered, the first thing that you would probably like to do is celebrate.

That's fine; you're entitled to one or two minutes of that.

But then the real work begins. You must immediately coordinate with your team to be assured that the deal is right for you and your career, and that it is still going to be financially and artistically rewarding.

As in the past, your team will assemble and begin to review the document with which you have been presented. You will discuss it in detail with them and work your way through all of the steps previously mentioned. You will be discerning in evaluating the project and will weigh all of its advantages and disadvantages, trying to understand how it will affect your career.

Regardless of the scope of the negotiations ahead, you are in the midst of a journey as an artist and professional. Make it a good one.

INSTANT REPLAY

Your career will be punctuated by different stages of development. If a development deal is prematurely terminated, it is important to maintain your focus until a new one is offered. In the interim, you should continue to work with your entire team to develop your career as you wait for opportunities to come again.

LITIGATION AND THE DEVELOPMENT DEAL

Litigation has become an unavoidable part of our lives in all aspects of business today.

Unfortunately, this is particularly true of the entertainment industry. In dealing with the industry, what should an artist do to prevent litigation and how can an attorney provide for preventive measures to reduce the possibility of litigation to its absolute minimum?

Boca Raton corporate and entertainment attorney Jan Michael Morris states, "While there is no way to guarantee that you will prevent litigation, there are measures that can be taken in order to make a transaction as 'bulletproof' as possible. The key is the attention to detail given to a transaction and assurances that all aspects of the transaction are structured so that nothing is left to the imagination."

Entertainment attorney Paul LiCalsi addresses the issue of protecting one's intellectual property rights in litigation and the importance of deciding when and how to act. "As a litigator, I am most often asked by clients about the protection of their rights in the context of infringements, rather than at the creation or contract stages. I advise clients to protect their rights vigorously, while at the same time strategically approaching enforcement. Any perceived infringement must be appraised in relation to its seriousness, the strength of the claim, and the cost of enforcement."

Though litigation can be beneficial in the protection of your rights as an artist, it can come at a cost in time and expense. Yet it is important to understand exactly what it means to you as an artist.

LITIGATION: ITS WORTH, EXPENSE, AND AVOIDANCE

The threat of litigation should always be treated seriously in the entertainment business.

Paul speaks of the degree to which counsel for the artist will have to act, depending on the circumstances. "Sometimes a strong 'cease and desist' letter will do, and sometimes extremely aggressive litigation will be called for. I always advise a client never to make a threat of litigation unless he or she is prepared to follow through on it. Always conduct a cost/benefit analysis which takes into consideration both the immediate infringement and the market's perception of your client's readiness to protect the intellectual property."

Paul also comments on the business end of the decision on action to take, stating, "A professional artist cannot avoid the fact that he or she is not just a creator but is also in business. And like any other business person, an artist must acquire a fundamental understanding of how that business works."

Paul feels a good entertainment lawyer should provide the information and counseling that will enable the client to understand in basic terms how the relevant industry is organized, how rights are protected and exploited, where the sources of income are, and all other relevant business issues, including litigation issues. Paul reminds us, "An artist needs to know a bit about the fundamentals of copyright, contracts, rights, and obligations. A good lawyer will not only draft and negotiate contracts, but will also help educate the client."

THE FACTS ABOUT LITIGATION

As an artist, you must understand the facts about litigation.

Kim Kolback discusses what the artist should do to prevent litigation and how the attorney can provide for preventive measures to reduce the possibility of litigation to its absolute minimum. "Unfortunately, for the financially challenged artist, the obvious answer for preventing litigation is that the artist needs to hire and pay a good entertainment attorney to make sure that any contractual obligation to be signed is fair and comprehensive from the 'get go.'"

Kim feels that in order to reduce the possibility of litigation, one of the best terms an attorney can put in a contract is an attorneys' fees clause. She states, "Most entertainment companies do not like these because the new artist can rarely afford to hire an attorney to prosecute or defend a case. However, if there is an attorneys' fee clause in the parties' agreement, the artist can almost always find a litigation attorney to take a good case, with the understanding that the litigation attorney will get paid under the clause."

Jan Michael Morris comments that litigation is an abstract term, and the costs and expense of litigation and the time involved will vary depending on the case. Jan claims that there are certain universal attributes of litigation that an artist must take into account any time litigation is threatened or commenced. In addition to the attorney's charges for time, litigation can be very costly.

Jan notes, "Hard costs of litigation can include costs for taking and transcribing depositions and retaining experts, paralegals, and other third parties to assess and evaluate the claims. In addition, there are abstract costs. For example, the amount of time expended by the artist in assisting in the litigation can be very significant, be it preparing for interrogatories, testimony at depositions, or assisting the professionals in preparing or otherwise pursuing the litigation."

Thus, Jan feels that the value placed on an artist's time can easily be more important than the value of the time expended by the professional serving the artist, because the time spent by an artist in litigation can be counterproductive to the artist advancing his or her career.

Jan also remarks, "There are other abstract costs of litigation to the artist's business and brand. Depending on the nature of litigation, its impact may be far-reaching. For example, if the artist is charged with a crime, the costs of the litigation go far beyond just dollars and cents. The impact of criminal litigation could have a disastrous effect on the artist's career. In that scenario, proper steps must be taken in order to mitigate the potential damage as a result of any adverse litigation." As you can see, the cost of litigation is far-reaching and encompasses more than just an attorney's time and out-of-pocket costs.

Dixon Dern weighs in on dealing with the possibility of litigation, commenting, "Because my practice is primarily of a transactional nature, I would normally refer the matter to trial counsel, advising the client, whether he or she is a plaintiff or defendant, to really work to get all the evidence in order, have all the arguments refined, and be certain that all other matters relating to litigation are handled. These are the same instructions I give to litigants when arbitrating their case."

Boca Raton corporate attorney Garry O'Donnell expresses his thoughts on the costs inherent in litigation. "While sometimes ego-satisfying and financially rewarding for trial lawyers, the bottom line is that litigation is often fatal to industry relationships, being costly and always over budget. It is also disruptive to conducting business and can expose the artist to public scrutiny. And it is unpredictable and subject to multiple reviews, revisions, and even reversal on appeal."

For those who feel the need to litigate, this is a matter that must be carefully and thoroughly discussed with the entertainment attorney and the rest of the team. Moreover, litigation is like a freight train. Once it begins to roll, it is very difficult to stop in short order. Thus, the benefits must clearly outweigh the detriments, and the result must be worth the effort in time and money.

THE ARTIST AS A TARGET FOR LAWSUITS

Certain artists often attract high-profile attention, sometimes resulting in high-profile suits.

Todd Brabec comments on the issues artists face in threatened or actual litigation, stating, "Unfortunately, the profile of artists in the entertainment industry many times invites the threat, whether real or imagined, of litigation. Putting aside the fact that lawsuits can always seem to come out of the woodwork, the best you can do is make your client aware of all of the various possibilities for litigation in his or her field and try to prepare accordingly." Todd adds that advice on a business structure that reduces liability is always important too, particularly regarding representing a celebrity in all aspects of a career.

And Emily Graham states, "There may be no fool-proof way to avoid litigation. But some good tips are to keep everything in writing and have your attorney look over everything before agreements are finalized." Emily tells us that there are so many aspects of the entertainment industry in play that it is practically impossible to foresee all potential pitfalls. However, she adds, "If you are faced with a litigation issue, either as a plaintiff or defendant, contact your attorney as soon as possible. It may be best to settle, but don't settle without first talking to your lawyer. Also, remember that Hollywood can be a small town, and litigation can and does ruin relationships. So be prepared."

Threats of lawsuits occur regardless of whether an artist maintains a high, middle, or low profile. The secret is to rely on your team and reduce such threats to their absolute minimum.

INSTANT REPLAY

The possibility of litigation must always be considered when negotiating a development deal. Your attorney can provide you with important knowledge about the business and legal aspects of the deal and the facts about litigation.

MEASURES TO PREVENT LITIGATION

As an artist, you can do your best to avoid litigation by knowing and understanding your business and legal adversaries.

Gregory Curtner discusses measures to reduce the possibility of litigation to its absolute minimum. "Avoid threats and 'take it or leave it' positions. Know your business partners and the opposing attorney. Maintain relationships and keep lines of communication open. Be prepared to litigate and win if necessary by having highly skilled litigation counsel ready." And in the event of litigation, Gregory tells us what he does to help prepare his clients for it. "Discuss all steps thoroughly and carefully to assure them it won't be as bad as they imagine, and that it will be fair in the end."

Nashville entertainment attorney Tim Warnock speaks about reducing the possibility of litigation to its absolute minimum. "For instance, with respect to litigation in copyright infringement, one of the most effective preventative measures is to document as specifically as possible the creative process. Work tapes, lyric sheets, appointment books, and other evidence of the creative process can prove very helpful in establishing independent creation of an allegedly infringing work."

Tim also notes, "Avoiding too much detail in describing influences and sources of inspiration may dissuade an otherwise litigious plaintiff from making a claim. With respect to issues arising from the interpretation of contracts or an artist's contribution to any particular project, detailed, accurate documentation is an important preventative measure."

Todd Brabec comments on preparing a client for litigation if it is inevitable. "My experience with litigation is that it is costly, time consuming, and a great distraction to an entertainer's career. But if one chooses to litigate, as in some cases there is no alternative, the artist must be positive as to the merits of the case but be reasonable as to the possible outcomes."

Always keep an open mind on litigation. Avoid it as much as you can. However, there is a time when litigation may be necessary in order to protect and enforce your rights under law and in equity. Your attorney can explain this aspect of law.

YOUR ATTORNEY AND YOUR TEAM TO THE RESCUE

Jan Michael Morris has other interesting thoughts about avoiding litigation. "There are a number of preventive measures that an artist can use to prevent or mitigate the possibilities of litigation in the future. The most important preventative measure is for an artist to have the proper professionals in place in order to properly manage his or her career. Such a career can be a complex paradigm, and, depending on the artist, there can be various aspects to that career."

Jan provides an example on point. "An athlete not only has a career in his or her particular sport, but an athlete's 'brand' may extend to merchandising, marketing, books, movies, the Internet, and other intellectual property deals which extend far beyond the playing field. Therefore, in order to prevent or mitigate the possibility of litigation, the artist must understand and accept that he or she cannot manage all aspects of a career without a core group of dedicated professionals, especially the participation of proper and experienced legal counsel."

And artists may need more than one attorney for expertise in different aspects of entertainment law.

Jan adds, "An artist may need a lawyer to handle the transactional aspects of the artist's career, including review and preparation of any and all contracts that he or she may need. Moreover, the professional advice of a litigation attorney may be required to handle aspects of litigation that are outside the expertise of the transactional attorney. Or the artist may need the advice of an attorney specializing in intellectual property rights or real property law. In this instance, with such varied and diverse media in the twenty-first century, it's critical that the artist's career and intellectual property rights are adequately protected."

YOUR TEAM AND LITIGATION

Your team can be all that stands between you and success or failure in litigation. This is particularly true in reducing the possibility of a lawsuit.

Jan discusses this issue. "The best way to mitigate or prevent litigation is to have the proper professional in place and on retainer in advance so that the artist's rights are protected. Some artists take it upon themselves to review their own contracts or otherwise avoid the assistance of the proper professionals, and this can be a ticking time bomb. There must be confidence in those professionals so that the artist is comfortable leaving matters outside his or her area of expertise to the proper professionals in order to avoid or mitigate the possibility of litigation. Most litigation occurs as a result of the artist's failure to retain the proper professionals to protect the artist's interest. The best defense is always a good offense, and having the proper professionals in place is an investment in the artist's future."

Paul LiCalsi speaks of the kind of advice an artist should receive from counsel in the event of litigation and how to deal with it. "After you've gotten all the facts, give your client, the artist, and your client's other professional advisors as clear and objective an appraisal of the claims as possible. In other words, how strong is the case? What level of commitment by the client will the litigation require, both in terms of the artist's personal involvement and financially? What are the risks and how will they be dealt with? How will the lawsuit affect the artist's public image? Are there strategic career issues that the litigation might affect that must be considered? All of these things must be considered and discussed."

Joseph Arrington talks of having a consciousness about litigation, stating, "From the beginning of their journey within the industry, the artist and his or her team should conduct each transaction with the possibility of litigation in mind and recognize it as a realistic component of doing business in entertainment, especially since litigation can both benefit and burden them."

Entertainment attorney John Bradley speaks about the need to understand litigation in order to avoid it. "The experienced entertainment litigator has the unique opportunity to envision litigation when drafting an agreement. With foresight, the attorney can work 'backward' and address the volatile issues which may arise, hopefully avoiding a range of potential problems in the future."

Dixon Dern comments on preventing litigation or reducing its possibility. "First, the attorney should be careful in reviewing or drafting contracts so that they are clear, concise, and understandable to all parties. For instance, if reviewing a long-form studio contract, it is a good idea to keep a checklist of points that have to be changed every time so that nothing is missed. Most contract actions arise because when a breach is alleged, the defense is that the contract means something other than what the claimant thinks it means."

And George Stein discusses the importance of proper writings in order to keep the possibilities of litigation to an absolute minimum. "Clear written agreements between the person or entity that controls the intellectual property rights and other third parties who will be involved in the exploitation of the rights will go a long way towards minimizing the need for litigation."

Your goal as the artist is to reduce your risks of litigation to an absolute minimum. Never forget that. And if you do, your attorney will in all likelihood remind you.

INSTANT REPLAY

The threat of litigation within the entertainment industry has become an integral part of doing business today. This is in part due to the high profile of artists and the nature of the business. Your attorney will be aware of the need to take preventive measures to reduce threats of litigation to their absolute minimum as you continue along your career path.

ALTERNATIVE DISPUTE RESOLUTION (ADR)

Alternative dispute resolution (ADR) is an area of the law that permits alternatives to litigation. ADR is generally provided for in most development deals in all genres in the industry.

But how important is ADR in avoiding litigation, how does it work, and how may it help the artist as he or she continues on the path upward in the new entertainment industry?

ADR: DOES IT WORK?

Does ADR really work?

Dixon Dern states, "Sure it works! If you arbitrate, litigation is practically foreclosed except in case of appeals, and if the arbitrator is careful and stays within the bounds of the authority given, a vacatur (a setting aside of an Order) is very hard to establish. In matters under collective bargaining agreements, arbitration is always involved, as a counterpart to a no-strike clause, and every union agreement in the industry provides for arbitration. In employment cases, I think it is often workable as well, although strict rules of fairness must be applied, which is the case out here in California."

On the other hand, Kim Kolback is not enamored with ADR in the avoidance of litigation. "I am not a fan of ADR and usually delete all ADR clauses from my agreements. It used to be fashionable, fast, and affordable, but now it is the equivalent of a hugely expensive court proceeding and is not always binding. The only upside of ADR in the entertainment industry is the fact that the arbitrator is generally more familiar with entertainment-related issues. However, I am not convinced that this is always good if you are representing the artist."

Kim feels that often a jury will side with the artist who was "taken advantage of" by the "big, bad, and greedy" entertainment company. She adds, "On the other hand, I am a huge fan of mandatory pre-litigation mediation. Often a dispute can be resolved simply by hearing out the other side. This is an affordable way to force parties to give thoughtful consideration to the merits of their dispute prior to jumping into litigation."

PREVENTIVE MEASURES

And what of the preventive measures inherent in alternative dispute resolution?

As to such measures, Dixon Dern comments, "I recommend an arbitration clause in those cases where appropriate. I do not recommend a two-step provision, where the parties are obligated to mediate first and if that fails, then they go to arbitration, because I think mediation should be voluntary and not forced, and if a party refuses to mediate it may be and in some cases has been argued that failure to mediate is a breach."

Dixon generally recommends using the arbitration law in California. "California has a very complete arbitration act, and I often refer to that act in my arbitration agreement rather than the rules of an agency so as to save costs, at least in cases where I believe the parties will be able to mutually select an arbitrator without having to go to court. But sometimes there is a really good reason to have an agency involved, such as the American Arbitration Association (AAA), because of its ability to handle cases and the adaptability of its rules. In those instances, I usually recommend that AAA be the tribunal."

Tim Warnock discusses the use of ADR, stating, "Many courts are now requiring ADR in advance of setting a trial date. In that instance, ADR does not avoid litigation but may provide a means to resolve litigation without the necessity of having to go to trial and without incurring the expense of preparing for trial."

However, Tim states that if one must litigate, one must be prepared for the possibility of success or failure, and settlement must be understood as an alternative to a trial.

Tim also observes, "Mediators frequently note that settlement, through ADR or otherwise, is the only way that a party can control the outcome of a dispute. Settlement also allows the parties to reduce the costs of litigation. Trials are expensive and the outcome of a trial is always uncertain in advance of the judge or jury reaching a decision. Some adversaries leave little choice but to go to trial if their demands are patently unreasonable, but most cases should and do settle short of a trial."

The general opinion is that ADR is desirable in order to avoid the pitfalls of litigation and to achieve a hearing in a venue that is more expeditious than spending time and money in court.

THE RISING COSTS OF LITIGATION VERSUS ADR

What of the comparison of litigation costs and ADR costs? Is ADR a less expensive alternative?

Tim Warnock remarks, "In terms of dispute resolution, the rising costs of litigation seem to result in more clients being interested in alternative forms of dispute resolution, such as mediation. Courts also seem to be deciding more matters on either motions to dismiss or motions for summary judgment, and fewer civil cases seem to actually go to trial."

Garry O'Donnell feels that mediation and ADR are very pivotal to settlement of a dispute. "In the absence of a negotiated resolution, a formal mediation process is the crucial last step before entering into the legal arena with all its uncertainties, disruptions, and costs. As with the negotiation process, pre-lawsuit mediation can be required under an agreement or conducted anytime with the consent of the parties." Garry has years of experience negotiating settlements through alternative dispute resolution. His message is clear on advising a client on ways to avoid disputes, stating, "Dispute avoidance can be promoted by including in the agreement an avenue for pre-dispute negotiation. We can require in the agreement that disagreements arising during the course of the relationship with an artist will be subject to a negotiation process."

Todd Brabec believes that arbitration and mediation are preferable in many cases to litigation. "Costs are more manageable and the decision making is normally quicker. In most cases, a fair and reasonable result can be achieved with less rancor between the parties. You would hope that it is a better way to resolve most disputes."

And Paul LiCalsi opines on the importance of alternative dispute resolution in avoiding litigation. "As a litigator, I have often made use of mediation for entertainment disputes. In my experience, its effectiveness heavily depends on the intelligence, knowledge, skill, and energy of the mediator. I find a good mediator can be extremely effective in breaking through to adverse parties whose lawyers have encouraged them to take unreasonable positions."

CANDIDATES FOR ADR

What types of disputes are appropriate for ADR?

Garry O'Donnell states that although there are certain types of disputes that may be perceived as being strong candidates for ADR—such as royalties, fees, payments, and credit for work and issues on copyright—any issue or claim that may result in litigation can benefit from the ADR process. "In fact, over 90 percent of all litigation is settled before trial. A very small percentage of the remaining disputes that go to trial are commercial cases. Why? In the high-stakes business world, good lawyers and savvy clients know this to be true: a gladiator mentality and macho chest beating often catapult a resolvable dispute into expensive scorch-the-earth discovery battles and litigation, when an agreement to exchange information may facilitate an early resolution of everything from major conflicts to minor misunderstandings."

And how is a dispute worked out on an informal basis?

Garry suggests, "A question or disagreement can be set out by one party in writing with a short period for the other party to respond. In the event written communication is not completely successful, the parties can be required to meet promptly, with or without representatives, at a mutually convenient time. During this informal meeting, the parties exchange information and negotiate in good faith in an effort to reach an equitable and mutually beneficial and acceptable solution."

How complicated are disputes?

Disputes can be personal, business, or legal in nature. Garry states, "On routine personal and business issues, the attorney should try to stay in the background, understand the dynamics of the problem, and counsel the artist on approaches to achieve a resolution through a process which facilitates the avoidance of future disputes. In this way, we hope to eliminate communication breakdowns going forward that could boil over into a legal matter."

THE GIVE AND TAKE OF NEGOTIATION
In other words, it all boils down to the give and take of negotiation.

Garry emphasizes this in his advice to clients. "The first response to a legal dispute, if at all possible, should be negotiation. This can take place within a framework constructed in an agreement or put in place as needed. The keys to successful negotiation are an open exchange of information, understanding the differences between your client and the other parties and assisting the artist in achieving important goals and maintaining the relationships underlying the agreement."

Moreover, Garry notes that any seasoned trial attorney will confess that he or she has lost cases that were projected victories and have won other cases that were snatched from the jaws of defeat. Thus, he feels that the artist should consider counsel that is experienced in ADR as a viable alternative to litigation. He also reminds us that ADR is available under various federal and state statutes.

Garry states that negotiation, mediation, and arbitration are all first-choice alternatives to litigation, particularly in the relatively small world of entertainment. "An artist is well counseled to use every reasonably available opportunity to avoid the hazards of litigation, which often leaves both sides unsatisfied, and commit to a more constructive path. The front end of contract negotiation is the best beginning for the artist to be proactive in receiving the benefits of ADR, should a dispute arise."

WORDS OF WISDOM ON DISPUTES

Finally, Garry provides his "words of wisdom" to the artist in the event a contractual or other dispute must be handled. "Choose your counselors carefully, especially attorneys. Make sure that your legal counsel understands the benefits of alternative dispute resolution."

You have been provided with a glimpse of the legal and business issues you will need to be aware of in litigation. The very best advice you can receive is to stay in regular touch with your team and pay particular attention to any warning signs that may indicate the need to bring in your attorney in order to make every reasonable attempt to prevent litigation or minimize any adverse effect if it occurs.

INSTANT REPLAY

Alternative dispute resolution, or ADR, has become very popular in resolving legal disputes without resorting to a lawsuit in court. This is in part due to the rising cost of litigation today. Though there are advantages and disadvantages to ADR, it can be an invaluable tool in the protection of your rights as an artist.

AND IT'S A WRAP

And it's a wrap, with some thoughts for your consideration.

Your team, led by your entertainment attorney, will assist you in reviewing and analyzing the elements of the development deal presented to you.

Your attorney will negotiate the terms and conditions of that deal in order to ensure it conforms to current industry standards and practices and meets your needs as an artist. Your development deal should be dynamic and permit you to enhance your opportunities for success within the industry.

It is important to protect your intellectual property rights, which may represent the most valuable aspect of your work. Litigation is a measure that should be considered in the enforcement of these legal rights under law. You should always seek advice from your attorney, who will assist you in protecting those rights and, in the process, measure the value of litigation against its expense as well as alternatives to litigation, such as mediation and alternative dispute resolution.

FILM

- ★ The development deal in film presents the opportunity for a budding director or producer to show the world the nature of their respective talents within the industry.
- ★ Obviously, your success will be built upon the strategic skills of your team. Use your team wisely and the world can be yours.

TELEVISION

- ★ Because of the shorter period of time typically allotted to the development of television programs, the window of opportunity may open more quickly than in film. However, it can close just as quickly.
- ★ Utilize the assistance of your team to take you into development deals, to maintain them, and to carry you to other deals that may be just around the corner.

MUSIC

- ★ As stated previously, the music industry has morphed to the extent that many artists and producers have now created their own development deals. In fact, many use social media to display their music and build a strong regional or even national and international audience for their music.

★ Nonetheless, whether such deals are independent or through the major record labels, they require a great deal of thought and planning in this ever-changing industry. There is no better time to use the skills of your team than at this period in your career.

THE LITERARY ARTS

★ The mainstream publishers offer development for writers in the form of book deals, providing for the author to create a number or series of works over a period of time. But the publishing industry is also moving through a spinning paradigm of changes. The road ahead may be challenging, but the rewards are well worth it.

★ Be prepared for deals to develop and change as the market changes. Even authors who take the independent path for publishing should expect change. It is now part of the literary landscape. In this instance, it is important to rely on your team for guidance and advice.

FASHION AND MODELING

★ Development deals in fashion and modeling are unique in that the public is looking for the next new look or great face to carry it.

★ As such, the deals will vary depending on the goals of the designer or model. In this case, the team's advice and expertise can help make the difference in the path to success.

THE VISUAL ARTS AND THE FINE ARTS

★ Development deals are defined differently in the visual arts and fine arts. In the visual arts, usually an artist will have his or her works exhibited in a gallery, subject to contractual arrangements negotiated through agents or legal counsel.

★ Regardless, the same rules of legal and business engagement apply. Use your team carefully because events can change rapidly, sometimes in the blink of an artist's eye.

TEAM HUDDLE

Your team will be critical in the successful negotiation of the development deal.

★ Your attorney will be your guiding light in the negotiation of the development deal, and you will also rely on the rest of your team to have a well-crafted and viable agreement. Of course, in the entertainment industry, most deals are subject to market conditions, the nature of the competition, and many other factors. Your team coordination will begin in earnest once your deal is signed.

★ Your talent manager will assist your attorney and the

other members of your team in analyzing and negotiating the development deal.

★ Your literary manager and writing coach will also provide insight into the artistic structure of the development deal.

★ Your agent will work closely with your attorney and producer in negotiating the development deal.

★ Your editor will be available whenever necessary and will coordinate with your literary manager and producer in the development deal.

★ Your producer may bring the development deal to the team or may assist in negotiating it, analyzing it from his or her artistic and business vantage

★ Your publicist will review the development deal from a public relations standpoint, and his or her feedback can be very important to the direction of your career based on that deal.

LIGHTS, CAMERA, ACTION!

With great effort, a little good luck, and the assistance of your entertainment attorney and your team, you'll begin to find the success you have sought.

The road is long and you have worked hard, following the advice and counsel of your entertainment attorney and others on your team along the way. Now you are there. But your work has not ended. It is just beginning, as you finally begin to discover success within the new entertainment industry.

A STORY INSPIRED BY A BROADCASTER, JOURNALIST, AND TELE-VISION PERSONALITY

The studio was bustling with action and movement as she sat in her chair on the set, while the line director began a final check for sound and lighting.

As she waited, she studied her interview questions for the guests that day. A crew member told her the taping would begin in about four minutes. She quietly reviewed her opening monologue in her notes and on the teleprompter.

As she waited, she glanced around the studio as the crew made their final preparations. Her on-air guests were waiting in the green room.

"Three minutes to taping!"

Her make-up artist scurried over and took a moment to apply just a bit of color to her cheeks to accommodate for the high definition cameras.

And she thought back to the time when she considered becoming a broadcast journalist, after a successful career in education, modeling, and motion pictures as an assistant film manager, reviewing scripts for a prominent Hollywood producer.

She recalled making the decision to pursue a career in broadcasting and studying the fundamentals of writing television broadcast copy, interviewing and reporting in the field, on-air anchoring, radio reporting, and television and radio production. She fondly remembered her internship at the news department of a major network-affiliated television station in South Florida, in one of the fasting growing markets in the country.

She would travel around the metropolitan area with the station's investigative team, then return to the newsroom and work right up until air-time, assisting in drafting and reviewing copy for the Emmy Award-winning anchors on the set.

"Two minutes to taping!"

She thought about how her efforts took her to another television network affiliate in the same market, and her initial meeting with the station owner. She spoke to him about her concept for a new television show that she would produce and host, containing in-depth interviews of celebrities in the world of entertainment, including motion pictures, television, music, and the arts, as well as the latest in breaking entertainment news, hot off the wire services. He was impressed with her and the idea, and the show became a reality, to be aired just before primetime programming every evening.

"One minute to taping! Ma'am, are you ready?"

She smiled. "Yes, I am."

After weeks of hard work in planning the set, lining up celebrity interviews, and piecing together the show format, she was just beginning to see her television show come into being.

"Ten seconds. Quiet on the set!"

She watched the line director hold five fingers up on his countdown, then four, three, two and one. The cameras rolled as she smiled and began to speak.

The television show is "Hello Hollywood," and the creator, producer, and on-air host is a broadcaster, journalist, and television personality.

She is René Katz.

And she is an artist.

SIX

AT LAST! SUCCESS IN THE
NEW ENTERTAINMENT INDUSTRY

Sailing o'er the water, whispering windless words
And wondering if they'll find a shore
Skies hazed blue beyond me,
seas glazed green go 'neath me
Gently rapping at my door.

Richard Warren Rappaport, "Sail Into the Sun,"
from the motion picture soundtrack of *Concert*

THE BASICS

This chapter is about the beginning of your newfound success in the entertainment industry and your quest to continue to maintain that success once you have reached the point at which you are beginning to develop a national reputation through your artistry.

The critical promotion of your image as an artist is discussed as well as the development of new business relationships within the industry while you continue to receive assistance, advice, and counsel from your team. The need to engage in time management is also examined as you maintain your vision and focus and find yourself delegating responsibilities to team members in order to make the best use of your working hours.

Lastly, the importance of the management and preservation of your wealth is addressed as you begin to attain financial security and look to create a strategy that will protect your money and assets as your career prospers.

WHY THIS CHAPTER IS IMPORTANT TO YOU

Your success in the industry is paramount. This chapter is about developing and maintaining it.

FILM

- ★ Hollywood is more than a name or a place. It is a state of mind, and that is what makes it so exciting. Success in this industry can begin and end with one movie release, or it can continue for an entire lifetime.
- ★ Great projects and talent will rise to the top and, with effort, hopefully remain there. If it is your film project, make it as good as you can.

TELEVISION

- ★ Television is a medium where a project can move in the fast lane, from the moment the ink is dry on a development deal to its network premiere.
- ★ This industry holds incredible promise for those who live within it and help to create award-winning programming.

MUSIC
- ★ The music industry today is constantly redefining and reinventing itself as the distribution system takes new and different forms.
- ★ Through it all, great songs and the artists who sing them will remain. As a musician, that is what is expected of you.

THE LITERARY ARTS
- ★ Success for authors never stops with publication of the first book. In fact, that is just the beginning.
- ★ Writing is perennial. It never ends. Be prepared to bring your stories to the world.

FASHION AND MODELING
- ★ Fashion is an industry in which designers are constantly on the move, looking for tomorrow's styles. Concepts evolving out of vintage clothing continue to live in new designs inspired by the past. Set your pace as a designer, and you can lead the pack.
- ★ And models are looking for the right fashions to make the right name at the right time on the world's runways.

THE VISUAL ARTS AND THE FINE ARTS
- ★ Many visual artists will tell you they find success in the creation of the work itself.
- ★ As a visual artist, you are expected to present your vi-

sion of reality as you see it. That makes your work very personal, introspective, and unique.

— THE COURT OF ARTISTIC OPINION —
"COUNSELORS, APPROACH THE BENCH"

The Court of Artistic Opinion is back in session. Once again, you are there with your entertainment attorney by your side and your team behind you.

As you observe the proceedings, you wonder what it was that brought you to this time and place, where you are now just beginning to taste the fruits of your labors. Your attorney will confirm that your hard work and dedication to your craft have finally begun to pay off, with the assistance of your team and perhaps a little good luck.

But finding success is only the beginning of the process. Maintaining success can be even more difficult. You have your attorney and your team. That's a great start!

With your legal and professional team in place, you are ready to break new ground in your career. Welcome to your newfound success!

THE ARTIST IN THE INDUSTRY

As the artist, you have entered that period when you have begun to move with your circle of friends and colleagues in the industry and are becoming known as an emerging professional in your particular genre. Though you will always have your team in place and ready to assist you at a moment's notice, it is important to remember that in the industry you may be your own best promoter.

In fact, as you travel through your business, professional, and social circles, you are judged on your demeanor, acumen, and conduct, as well as your commitment to the causes and projects you espouse. Thus, you must always try to maintain a presence that demonstrates to others that you are courteous, confident, and focused. This is especially important because in public, everything that you do and all that you say will affect how others within the industry judge you.

And you must of course continue to remain true to your art. For that is what brought you here.

PROMOTING YOUR IMAGE AND DEVELOPING PROFESSIONAL RELATIONSHIPS

In terms of the general promotion of your image, it is important that you speak individually and collectively with your team in order to fashion a strategic plan for the continued development of your career.

In this regard, you should continue to look to the expertise of your attorney, publicist, manager, agent, and other members for the proper guidance and help. Once you have done that, you can then begin to work with them to refine your course of action as you move forward.

Though there are many ways you can develop your reputation in the industry, one particularly effective method is for you to engage in interviews or public speaking, either at gatherings or in the media, such as radio, television, streaming feeds on the Internet, or other social media. Such speaking engagements may be scheduled by your publicist in conjunction with the company with which you are involved.

Understanding the art of public speaking is rather important and is in itself a skill to be learned and refined. If you have not studied speaking in public, your publicist can probably assist you in preparing so that you can develop this skill. And such a skill can become significant to you as your career continues to grow.

Notwithstanding the potential cause you may espouse or the venue at which you may be asked to speak, it will be helpful to be able to have the confidence to deliver your thoughts and views to others.

HOORAY FOR HOLLYWOOD! ADVANCING YOURSELF IN THE FILM INDUSTRY

Entertainment attorney Peter Dekom provides advice for the successful artist in the motion picture industry, whether he or she is an actor, director, producer, or other professional, in maintaining his or her position and stature in the entertainment industry.

Peter's comments are intriguing. "Actors, be aware of the film as a whole, not just the role. Understand that the current market is looking for escape and avoids serious issues like the plague. Until the economy improves, go with the flow. Take chances. The least sustainable career in features is the leading man or leading woman."

And why are those careers the least sustainable? Peter states, "In a 'what's cool next' universe, established leading men and women have a life expectancy of three films among the cherished 15 to 25 age group. Character actors, those who can make us laugh or entertain us with 'over-the-top' personalities, have vastly more sustainability because they are constantly providing us with 'new' characters. And be a tad mysterious. Beware of celebrity overexposure."

As for those intrepid film and television directors, Peter has these suggestions. "Regardless of success, direct as if your career depends on your next effort. It just might!"

With tongue in cheek, Peter comments, "If you hold back anything, your audience will know and leave the theater with a bad taste in their mouths. Take them where they have never been, push the envelope, give them a great ride and cinematic moments they will remember, keeping in mind that at least six of those moments per film have to be perfect. Paint amazing characters—even your villains should have three-dimensional personalities—and give them a compelling story!"

Regarding our creative authors and screenwriters, Peter offers these salient observations. "Never before has the film industry been as dependent on the efforts of writers. Write, rewrite, torture yourself, get input from tough critics, and rewrite. Use all of your connections on the planet to get your stuff read. And if you are established, except for sequels, be different, be compelling, and learn how to surprise and amaze." But even though writers rule, Peter adds, "You have one of the most difficult jobs on earth, and you will be underappreciated even when you deliver."

And for the producers, Peter suggests, "It's the material, it's the material, it's the material, it's the material, it's the material, it's the material . . . and the political wisdom to know what to do with it!"

What is gleaned from this is that writing for film is a learned skill. The industry accepts all those who wish to learn and applauds those who make the attempt to develop their skills. And your team will assist you in accomplishing that.

INSTANT REPLAY

Promoting your image and developing business relationships may define the success and length of your career. Work closely with your team to promote your business and artistic relationships.

MANAGING YOUR TIME

Managing your creative time may be one of the most significant things you do as an artist. Your time during the working day can be very limited. And you have an obligation to yourself, to your friends and colleagues, and to your team to utilize that time wisely and judiciously.

DELEGATING RESPONSIBILITIES

Now that success is beginning to define your career track, you will want to consider what projects and causes deserve your time. This is especially true because, you may be surprised to find that such causes, regardless of how important they are to you, may take excessive amounts of your time, perhaps even more than you should allocate to them.

Author Steve Alten underscores the reasons for delegating time-consuming activities. "I put a lot of pressure on myself to keep new projects in the pipeline. As a writer, I'm sort of on my own island. I stick with a daily routine, and when I'm writing a book, I work six to seven days a week. Success relies on hard work."

Thus, in order to make the correct decisions on how to use your time wisely, you should coordinate with your team. Your talent or literary manager can coordinate with your agent and publicist to assist you in planning your business day when it comes to taking on projects or causes. Typically, you would be involved in meetings once a week, preferably in the early part of the week, in order to maintain an organized schedule.

Your attendance at these meetings is important because you should be able to determine the extent and nature of your schedule for the weeks ahead. Such meetings can generally be conducted at your home or office, or at your manager's office.

During the meetings, you will have the opportunity to examine and evaluate projects, including causes, charitable, political, and otherwise, that are of interest to you or that may be presented to you and your team. With respect to such projects, please remember that once you begin to attain the status of a rising star within your industry, you will, in all likelihood, be flooded with requests to become involved in business deals; to attend social, charitable, or political events; or to donate your money to certain causes.

It will be practically impossible for you to be screening or handling all such requests. That is essentially the responsibility of your team. Thus, it is important that you be aware of the projects being presented to you so that you remain in the loop and have a say in all decisions regarding these solicitations.

And if your team makes initial decisions that will involve you in any project with your advice and consent, it is imperative that your attorney review all material associated with that project in order to ensure that it is legitimate and worthy of pursuing; that it is in compliance with all applicable laws, rules, and regulations; and that your involvement in it will not subject you to unnecessary liability.

Once you have established which projects or charitable, civic, or other causes to pursue, your entire team can move forward to assist you in planning your schedule so that you will properly allot your time. Developing a career takes time and, as discussed before, vision and focus. In this regard, as you begin to taste success within the industry, it is imperative that you maintain your vision and focus, which also helps to preserve your artistic integrity and direction.

VISION, FOCUS, AND SUCCESS

At this point in your career, vision and focus can become absolutely critical for the continued attainment of success.

Entertainment attorney George Stein speaks about continued vision and focus, feeling it closely follows talent as one of the core attributes of a successful artist. George comments, "The artist should have a clear sense of who he or she is as a creative person and what he hopes to achieve and why. Fans gravitate to artists who have confidence in their vision of themselves and a strong sense of what they are trying to achieve artistically."

Likewise, the creative and business teams working with an artist are motivated to work harder for those artists and clients who have an artistic sense of themselves and exude the self-confidence associated with strong vision and focus.

And entertainment attorney Joseph Serling provides a suggestion for artists who are finding success, expressing the need for a careful business analysis of all existing contractual obligations as well as a review of the team that helped get the artist there, including management, the agent, the business manager, and the lawyer, in the event that personnel changes need to be made.

An artist's vision and focus may be important keys to longevity in his or her career.

Entertainment attorney and author Todd Brabec tells us the artist should continue to maintain focus but be prepared to modify it if necessary. "Don't be afraid to modify your vision if it will help you get to the place you want to be. You really need to be aware of what the business requires of you and what the market is for what you want to do and have to offer. You don't have to follow the crowd or emulate the trends to succeed, but you do have to put your vision into some type of perspective, or you could choose to be the solitary monk on the mountaintop singing songs to the animals and wind. That's fine if this is what you want."

When combined with imagination and creativity, as well as great teamwork and delegating one's time properly, there is no limit to your success within the industry.

INSTANT REPLAY

Perhaps one of the most important actions you can take is to delegate your time wisely. Optimize your time by utilizing your team properly, relying on the expertise of your team members. In this manner, you can continue to focus on your vision and your plans for the future.

MANAGING AND PRESERVING YOUR WEALTH

For most aspiring individuals in the entertainment industry, it may seem a bit premature to speak about needing the advice of a tax attorney or a wealth-management specialist. But it is never too early to begin to learn about the need for such assistance and how you can begin to develop and protect your asset base as you begin to develop your career.

WEALTH MANAGEMENT

Wealth management, simply defined, deals with the world of financial planning and the creation and management of an investment portfolio in order to maintain, protect, and develop wealth. A specialist in wealth management can work with you to provide an initial understanding of the importance of planning for your future. Such a specialist can discuss estate planning and other available tax benefits in order to reduce the risk of depleting your financial resources and keep your acquired wealth for your family and future generations.

Wealth-management specialists may be certified financial planners or have degrees in financial planning. And many wealth-management specialists are also attorneys. Regardless, the best approach is to utilize the services of the wealth-management specialist and to also seek the advice of a tax and estate attorney when needed.

Thus, by relying on the expertise of both, you can be apprised of the legal and business aspects of wealth management and be aware of the best course of action to take in protecting assets. In essence, you must understand this very critical aspect of developing and accumulating wealth, even before it exists.

TAX LAW AND WEALTH PRESERVATION

What is the entertainment lawyer's role in the preservation of wealth for a client?

Miami corporate and tax attorney Michael Axman states that the entertainment lawyer plays a vital role in assisting his clients in the areas of tax and wealth preservation, whether the artist is emerging or successful within the entertainment industry. "These are extremely important topics to be considered when representing clients, particularly sports figures, whose professional lives may only span a few years but whose earnings may need to sustain them for their lifetimes. This contrasts with most people, whose professional lives may span 30 or more years."

And artists, who may have longer careers than athletes, must still act to preserve their wealth early on. Thus, the planning process is important regardless of the artistic career.

Michael comments on such planning. "Planning recommendations are made based upon the individual facts and circumstances of the artist. Indeed there can be no 'broad brush' approach to planning. A client interview and estate planning questionnaire are essential to determine both the client's personal situation (single, single with children, married, married with children, divorced, divorced with children, creditor issues, special needs situations, elderly parents and infirmed dependents) and the potential avenues to the creation of wealth (employment contracts, licensing and merchandising agreements, copyrights, and trademarks)."

Michael also states that as a general rule, setting up a plan to protect future assets for someone with very little present wealth is, in general, easier than trying to preserve the wealth of a successful artist. "When dealing with the successful artist, the approach to the preservation and protection of the client's current wealth and future income will again be dictated by the facts and circumstances of the particular artist. Protecting wealth from current or future creditors is a difficult, sometimes impossible task, primarily handled by asset and creditor protection specialists and, as such, while important for the entertainment lawyer to understand, dabbling in the area is not recommended."

Thus, as an artist, your entertainment attorney must know when to bring in wealth management counsel specialized in this area of the law. Your career may depend on it.

TAX VEHICLES

And are there particular tax vehicles that an artist would find important in protecting income and investments?

Michael remarks, "Again it depends on the individual's circumstances, but, at the most basic level, the artist should have certain estate planning documents in place. First and foremost would be a pour-over will and a revocable trust. The primary function of the pour-over will is to name guardians for any minor children. The guts of the will are actually contained in the revocable trust, which, if funded during the artist's lifetime, can afford the client's family with a fairly easy transition of wealth and, more importantly, privacy, since assets held in the revocable trust do not pass through an expensive and very public state court probate proceeding."

Michael also feels that an irrevocable trust is often used for both asset protection reasons and for tax savings. "In situations where the trust holds life insurance on the life of the artist, if the trust is properly structured, the proceeds of the life insurance policy or policies owned by the trust, which may be substantial, can escape estate and generation-skipping taxes in the estates of the artist, his spouse, and his children."

Planning vehicles can make the difference for an artist. Once again, real expertise is essential.

REDUCING YOUR RISK OF EXPOSURE

At all times, you must consider reducing your overall risk to exposure.

Michael raises the importance of this general understanding of tax and wealth-management aspects of the entertainment industry. "If the artist wants to open a restaurant in his or her name, he or she needs to know that an investment vehicle such as a limited liability company must be formed to handle the venture so that, in the event the venture turns out to be a loser, the entity will go out of business, but the artist's personal liability would be limited to his or her investment. That is, the artist's accumulated and future wealth is not at risk as a result of this investment choice. A well-crafted prenuptial agreement can go a long way toward resolving many difficult ownership and valuation issues, such as issues dealing with copyrights, trademarks, merchandising agreements, pensions, etc., which can and do arise when the artist and his or her spouse decide to call it quits."

This applies regardless of whether plans call for following traditional methods of breaking into the industry, such as signing with a film or television production company or music label, or proceeding as an independent artist and raising funds for a project through friends and family or a private offering.

A STRATEGY FOR WEALTH

When and how should you create a strategy for wealth preservation? In essence, though you may not feel it is necessary or appropriate to plan management of funds that do not yet exist, it is important to be aware of such management for the future, when your wealth develops.

Tax specialist Martin Cass, CPA, explains, "A plan is always needed. In the entertainment and sports industries, where contracts dictate income levels, budgeting your money and knowing how much to put away is critical, so that at the end of your contract, you will have a certain amount of your income being invested at a conservative rate." Marty feels that the artist should always have his or her money at work making money and accumulating wealth.

West Palm Beach corporate and tax attorney and author Lazaro (Laz) Mur also has advice for the artist who wishes to be aware of a strategy for preservation of wealth. "Choosing the business entity used to be simple. It was primarily based on avoiding double taxation. Today, it also involves elements of asset protection, estate planning, and strategies to raise capital."

Laz feels that the choice of an experienced accountant is important because most of the research and development cost of a screenplay, manuscript, or music, film, or television production may be tax deductible, if properly documented. "That is where a qualified certified public accountant can make a big difference. Equally as important is to have a solid accounting and bookkeeping system in place."

Laz suggests that the entertainment attorney and tax attorney work together to develop a structure for the emerging entrepreneur at the time of inception of a creative idea in order to not only help protect future assets from the reach of creditors, but help reduce estate and gift tax exposure in the future. Such a structure is known as a Third Party Directed Beneficiary Trust, Dynasty Trust, or 678 Trust. These types of trust are best implemented before the particular entertainment venture goes into development so as to maximize

the benefits and minimize the costs. In this manner the assets held
by the 678 Trust would be beyond the reach of creditors, as would
the proceeds from a private annuity. Thus, in the event of death,
those assets would not be included in the estate.

YOUR ATTORNEY'S ROLE

Laz also believes that an experienced entertainment attorney is
critical, especially when working with the tax attorney and accountant, because he or she can take you from the point of conception
of a creative idea through development of the idea into a tangible,
valuable concept that can then be taken to development. And the
entertainment attorney will help the emerging entrepreneur understand and negotiate every aspect of the book or film contract.
"Typically, the entertainment attorney and tax attorney will work
with the entrepreneur to find the most suitable structure to carry
out the contemplated business plan. Once the business plan is fully
implemented and the book or film deal is closed and the money
starts flowing in, they can continue working with the emerging entrepreneur to address income tax planning issues as well as income
tax planning options."

THE TAX PLANNER

Michael S. Leone, CPA, JD, LLM, is an expert in tax planning for
high net worth individuals. Although Mike addresses tax planning for those artists who have begun to make money as their
career blossoms and who have sufficient income to focus on managing it, he also knows that it is important to be aware of the
eventual need for tax planning. In this regard, once the artist is

generating sufficient income, Mike suggests that he or she seek the advice of a tax planner on the proper steps to take to manage his or her money.

However, Mike cautions that nothing is simple in tax law, and one must be careful because it is not possible to have all rights to something without being taxed on it immediately. He feels that there must be some sort of income-deferral mechanism, citing as an example a tax vehicle titled the Rabbi Trust. This is an unfunded and unsecured nonqualified deferred compensation arrangement, in which the artist's employer sets up a trust and places assets in it to eventually pay the entertainer, athlete, or author at some future date. However, Mike states that the downside is that in the interim, the assets in that trust are subject to the claims of the employer's creditors if the employer becomes insolvent.

Another type of income is endorsement income. One of the ways to minimize taxes for such income is to create a separate legal entity to receive the income and then reduce that income by applying certain expenses, such as travel, entertainment, promotion, and professional fees. In this case, Mike feels that the artist may want to use his or her own company and deduct these expenses as a true business.

Mike also talks about a qualified retirement plan, available for one who creates his or her own business. Such individual plans should be the subject of discussions with your tax planner.

ASSET PROTECTION

Mike discusses wealth protection achieved through asset protection and protection from creditors. This pertains to making sure the entertainer or athlete has adequate insurance coverage for liability, such as umbrella coverage. He reminds us that the artist may also want to protect assets based on ownership and how such assets are titled. In such an instance, one can use domestic or foreign asset protection trusts, a limited liability partnership or company, or invest in annuity products, depending on the state. Moreover, prenuptial or postnuptial agreements can be very significant. It is also important to try to avoid personal guarantees of the debts of a business or investment entity.

Needless to say, Mike reiterates that it is vitally important to consult with a knowledgeable tax specialist in order to determine the proper path to take in managing your business affairs in the industry. And, as stated earlier, although the emerging artist may not have sufficient income to be immediately concerned about tax planning, it is just as important to be aware of its significance for the day when it will be needed.

Though the above constitutes just a brief summary of some techniques and vehicles to be used in the management and preservation of your wealth, it is always wise to seek the advice of a qualified tax attorney and certified wealth management planner to craft a personal strategy.

And the sooner you are properly structured, the better you will protect your assets and minimize the tax consequences of a profitable entertainment industry venture.

> **INSTANT REPLAY**
>
> Wealth preservation and management are crucial elements in the development of your career. Though you may not have wealth when you begin your career, you must understand how to handle and protect your money when you begin to generate income.

AND IT'S A WRAP

And it's a wrap, with some thoughts for your consideration.

Once success begins to make its mark upon your career, it will be important to promote your image and further develop your business relationships in the industry.

During this time, as with all other times during your work in the industry, you should be speaking individually and collectively with your team in order to continue to fashion a strategic plan for the path ahead.

You should be aware of the management and preservation of your wealth, seeking the opinions of experts in the field on ways to maintain and grow your wealth during your many years of success.

FILM

★ As you begin to clearly establish a reputation within the motion picture industry, it is essential to begin to manage both your time and your wealth. Your time becomes more important and precious because of the need to continue to focus on that next great picture.

★ Your wealth preservation is critical because it permits you to enjoy and maintain the financial rewards you have received and are continuing to earn. Work closely with your team as you develop as an artistic force to be reckoned with in the industry.

TELEVISION

★ Success in this industry can strike very quickly, and you must work hard to hold onto it and develop it. This is particularly true because of the immediacy of television and the speed at which your reputation may emerge.

★ As in film, you must manage your time and wealth for the future.

MUSIC

★ In this incredibly diverse and changing field, you should be very aware of the management of your time and rely upon your team to assist you in that endeavor.

★ The management of your savings can be critical given that many artists, because of time constraints, are focused on developing their careers with frequent performances and recordings and must have others assist them in preserving their wealth.

THE LITERARY ARTS

★ Your reputation as a writer can be established with the sale of your first book and may propel you into the highest level of literary fame. Always look ahead for that next great story and manage your time accordingly.

★ At the same time, use the expertise of your team to understand the importance of wealth management and preservation.

FASHION AND MODELING

★ The fashion world relies on the importance of time management, when minutes on the runway can make or break a young designer's career.

★ Success can come quickly in these industries. You must be prepared for it and plan for your financial future at the same time, protecting the money that you have worked so hard to earn.

THE VISUAL ARTS AND THE FINE ARTS

★ Visual artists who are focused on their works often do not have the time to manage their schedules or their wealth, and can use the assistance of their team. Work with your team to ensure the best use of your time.

★ The visual arts require the same degree of concentration as all other fields, and time and wealth management are equally as important.

TEAM HUDDLE

Your team will assist you in managing your time as you begin to find success in your chosen field.

★ Your attorney can be very helpful in counseling you in the management of your time as your career continues to unfold. And he or she can be crucial in providing advice as you speak with other members of your team about the building and management of your wealth.

★ Your talent manager will be aware of the importance of your time and may screen projects that come to your attention so that your time is properly utilized.

★ Your literary manager and writing coach may also assist in screening material presented to you by others.

★ Your agent will continue to look for opportunities for you within the industry as your career moves into fast-forward.

★ Your editor may assist your literary manager in preparing synopses or summaries of potential projects for you to review.

★ Your producer will also look for opportunities on your behalf or will review prospective projects as they come through the door.

★ Your publicist will review all serious inquiries from a public relations standpoint to ensure that such opportunities conform to the direction in which your career will be moving.

LIGHTS, CAMERA, ACTION!

You have found artistic and commercial success within the entertainment industry. Now it is time to speak of the responsibility of artistic leadership that comes with success.

A STORY INSPIRED BY AN AUTHOR AND HER BOOK

She had wanted this story to be original and intriguing. She wanted to let her imagination soar.

She had developed one of the most successful vintage clothing and accessories showrooms in the United States, creating a store that is a quarter of a city block in size and offering some of the finest pieces in the world, with items dating back over a century.

And although she came to work practically every day of the year, she found that she was never bored, never tired, always enlightened, and constantly challenged to make her business the very best in the world of vintage designer and couture fashion.

She appreciated the fact that the fashion in her store was a part of someone's history. She would often say that every article of clothing or accessory had a story, and that each story involved the personal lives of the people who wore the items.

At a point in time, she decided that she wanted to write about her experiences in the world of fashion and vintage clothing. But what would the theme be? She thought about it.

As she developed a storyline, she planned to write a book about the personal significance of vintage clothing to the individuals who wore them. She wanted to combine a sense of reality, drama, and mysticism that would blend the clothing and people with the ages.

She would focus her writings on a series of short stories of the people behind the clothing, whether they were consignors or purchasers.

Regardless, everyone in her book would have a story as they passed through the doors of her showroom. Though she had great ideas for these stories, she knew that she would need an editor to assist her and provide oversight for her writings.

She found an entertainment attorney and excellent editor and began to write; the stories unfolded as she wrote them down.

After a period of time, she completed the first full draft of her series of stories, and her editor reviewed them as a manuscript, looking for stories that were page turners: original, dynamic, and very readable.

Just as important, she would strive to create flowing dialogue and content that would ignite the reader's imagination.

As she began to complete the manuscript, she noticed that each character took on a life of his or her own, existing as if they were real people in real situations, looking for real answers.

When she finished, she had found what she was seeking.

She now understood that it was not so much that she was writing a book, but that she was telling stories and making the characters come alive. And it was dynamic, original, and enlightening.

Her published book is titled *The Truth of Time.*

She is Madeleine Kirsh.

And she is an artist.

SEVEN

YOU AND THE WORLD OF ENTERTAINMENT: ARTISTIC LEADERSHIP, THE POWER OF CELEBRITY, EDUCATION AND MENTORING, AND CHARITABLE AND CIVIC INVOLVEMENT

This city's filled with the shadows of people
who've lost their dreams
And only time will tell us if we're everything we seem
And I will love and care for you,
For as long as you want me to
And New York City smiles on you
My Ballerina.

Richard Warren Rappaport, "Ballerina,"
from the motion picture soundtrack of *Concert*

THE BASICS

This chapter is about your direction as a successful artist while you receive critical, artistic, and commercial acclaim within the entertainment industry. Also discussed are your leadership in the industry and the new responsibilities that await you as a result of that leadership. The power of your celebrity is analyzed as well as the merger of leadership and celebrity and the obligations this may bring.

The importance of maintaining proper social and professional industry contacts is reviewed, including a discussion on celebrity etiquette and its relevance to the world of entertainment.

Lastly, the significance of education, mentoring, and charitable and civic involvement in your community is analyzed as your fans, the industry, and perhaps the world look to you to demonstrate true leadership to others who are just beginning their careers. In this regard, how you may exercise your power of celebrity will demonstrate your commitment to the arts and to those around the globe who idolize and respect you.

WHY THIS CHAPTER IS IMPORTANT TO YOU

The world of entertainment shares the stage with and shines the spotlight on those who are involved in artistic leadership, including civic and charitable causes. Many in the industry consider it an obligation to help others.

FILM

★ Practically every successful individual in the motion picture industry is involved in leadership, education and mentoring, and charitable and civic involvement. It is considered part of giving back to your community and industry.

★ Your colleagues will respect the assistance and leadership you provide.

TELEVISION

★ As in film, professionals who work in the television industry are also heavily involved in roles of leadership, education, mentoring, charity, and civic affairs.

★ As in film, you are entering an area where involvement in such causes has become the norm and part of the professional landscape.

MUSIC

★ Music, civic affairs, and charitable causes go together. All the national professional academies, including The Recording Academy, are supportive of these causes. Your support is welcome and expected.

★ And as in film and television, artists and other professionals in the music industry feel they have an obligation to help others. Simply put, it is what people in this industry accept as part of their professional and personal commitment.

THE LITERARY ARTS

★ Many authors and publishers are supportive of causes in the literary arts.

★ Their involvement in outreach programs and projects helps to strengthen the industry and provides a literary forum. As an author, your words may change the world in the support of causes you espouse.

FASHION AND MODELING

★ The fashion and modeling industries have always been supportive of civic and charitable endeavors.

★ These industries have become synonymous with such causes, and that is good because it reflects a commitment to help others. Your commitment can make the difference for those in need.

THE VISUAL ARTS AND THE FINE ARTS

★ Visual artists and gallerists have supported causes and have become an integral part of the community, supporting others through their art.

★ It is this support that brings attention to worthy causes and charities. Visual art represents the artist's window to the world. You are sharing your artistic vision with others, and you can also show your appreciation by helping those less fortunate.

— THE COURT OF ARTISTIC OPINION —
"COUNSELORS, APPROACH THE BENCH"

This is the final session of the Court of Artistic Opinion for today. And again, your entertainment attorney is by your side.

Your attorney will tell you that involvement in civic affairs, charitable causes, and mentoring is important because it gives you the opportunity to give back to your community and the industry. And both opposing counsel and the court will unanimously agree.

That is artistic leadership. You have an obligation to demonstrate that type of leadership when you are heading toward the top.

And it is the proper and courageous thing to do.

You are a leader in your art, in your field, and in your heart. That is what makes you a true artist who has found artistic and commercial success in the new entertainment industry.

ARTISTIC LEADERSHIP

Leadership as an artist is often coupled with success. And it is imperative that you understand how to deal with success and use it to your greatest advantage.

Television personality Ingrid Hoffman was asked how she remains open to the feelings and beliefs of others as a successful television personality. "I believe in humbleness and kindness and we are so in need of more of this." Speaking about ego in the industry, Ingrid states, "Check it at the door. After all, we're only just cooks. Look, none of the super chefs I know has invented the cure for cancer, so in my eyes we are not above the rest."

Producer and literary manager Ken Atchity feels that, though it is important to advise his clients who are writers on how to handle success when they find it, sometimes it can be dizzying for those who are new to the field. In other words, dealing with success depends on the individual.

We must all remember that great stories and great art belong to the world. Such creative ideas should be shared with others so that they may appreciate and enjoy them, as well as learn from them. Thus, it should be your goal to create art that challenges and inspires. And like all good things, that requires time and thought.

THE POWER OF CELEBRITY

To walk the streets of Los Angeles is to be in a town that is one of the crown jewels in the world of motion pictures, television, music, and the arts.

Of course, it is true that great talent exists around the globe and is found in practically every country. However, only certain cities may stake a claim to be true centers of entertainment and the arts, and Los Angeles is the city that sits at the top of that list, exuding a sense of power and style that defines it as the heart of the industry. You are now a successful player in the industry and are just beginning to receive critical acclaim, recognition, and wealth. All this reflects a growing awareness of your presence as an accomplished artist in your industry.

And how should you handle your newfound fame? Will you become overconfident and expect special treatment? Will you feel that you are entitled? In other words, will you begin to believe your own hype? Understanding your role as an artist and reminding yourself of your career path is critically important at this time.

Producer and broadcaster René Katz believes that individuals in this industry should always remain grounded and focused on their work. "You should continue to hone your craft, whatever it may be. The competition is fierce, not just on a weekly basis, but on a daily basis." René feels that by maintaining your focus and continuing to take on projects that are challenging and inspiring, you remain artistically, intellectually, and emotionally strong.

And why does your celebrity exist? René states, "Your celebrity exists solely because of your talent, drive, hard work, dedication, commitment, and perseverance, not in spite of it. People will admire you for those qualities. And don't be surprised if they expect you to continue to be successful."

You are beginning to see the results of very hard work and commitment to your art. Now you can begin to understand and experience the incredible power of celebrity.

THE CRITICAL ACCLAIM FOR YOUR WORK

Author George Rios comments on the power of celebrity by simply stating, "In my world of writing, if you ask if your message will carry further if you become famous, then the answer is, 'absolutely it will.' But, one is always in the hands of fate, and your focus should lie with the quality of what you write."

Will your rise to stardom be fleeting, and will people then forget you? Is the axiom true that you are only as good as your last project in Hollywood? René Katz remarks, "As an artist, you should always look for new frontiers in your work and be prepared to expand upon your craft. Again, remember that the projects upon which you are working are always in flux and that is expected. What is important is that you are striving, and that is timeless."

And how should you harness the power of celebrity once you begin to have it? Entertainment attorney Emily Graham states, "Celebrity is a fleeting Zeitgeist that should be roped and wrestled like a bull. If not, it will get away as quickly as it roared into the stadium. Make sure you have and trust your publicist, manager, and agent to capitalize on the moment. For that, you must look within yourself and return to your core values; the values that you began to develop when you were younger, before the fame and fortune became a reality and brought you to New York City or Los Angeles and the industry."

You must understand those values for which you stand. You should look to your belief system and remember why you wanted to be in the industry in the first place. You came to live your dream. The corollary to this belief is that, as an artist, you exist as a creative force, regardless of the genre in which you work. The opportunity to become recognized within your field is simply the start of your career, not the middle or end of it.

In order to continue your climb to success, you should always think of your beliefs which brought you here, and internalize them. They will carry you through the exciting and productive periods as well as the periods during which you may be in transition with regard to your art and work.

SUCCESS AND CELEBRITY

Are success and celebrity two distinct concepts?

Screenwriter Robin Abramovitz Goldberg feels that being successful and being a celebrity are obviously very different. "As a writer, I want to find success based upon my hard work, dedication, and determination to create a story that incorporates many valuable qualities of life." And Robin wants others to enjoy her story. To her, success is defined as seeing that her work is appreciated. Yet she feels that celebrity is a by-product of success, in that it represents the accolades one receives within the industry based on such success.

Psychologist Dr. James Huysman speaks about the challenges faced by the artist who becomes a celebrity and the pressure of adjusting to it, speaking of avoiding the "crash and burn" scenario that occurs so frequently in Hollywood and the industry. "The artist as a celebrity must have a method, procedure, or process by which to deal with success."

Jamie feels that the incredible power of the camera provides an external reinforcement for the artist's own self-esteem and can create an artificial and inflated view. In essence, the fame becomes a drug. "We can push away from our real selves and replace it with the 'persona' of a celebrity. Of course, the worst thing that you can do is to embrace your own hype and become a celebrity in your own mind. Just as young people can feel they are immortal, celebrities can believe they are eternal. What is important is that the artist as a celebrity remains 'grounded' in family, true relationships, friends, and therapy if necessary."

We must believe in the artistry of life and the creativity inherent in one's art. It is the art that speaks within us that must be nurtured. And true artistic success lies in the artist's ability to have a clear vision of his or her role in art for the entire world to enjoy, as well as in being a role model for others to follow.

> **INSTANT REPLAY**
>
> Artistic leadership is essential to maintaining one's reputation in the entertainment industry. The power of celebrity, when coupled with leadership, may give you the ability to achieve greater success and continue to create your art while receiving critical acclaim and establishing new artistic frontiers.

WHEN LEADERSHIP AND CELEBRITY MERGE

There is a point and time in your career when leadership and celebrity merge. The result can be incredibly powerful, depending on how you utilize them. When leadership is combined with celebrity status, one individual can reach great numbers of people and accomplish great things, whether it is for education and mentoring, charity, or civic affairs.

CELEBRITY AND RESPONSIBILITY

Author Steve Alten states that celebrity brings a great deal of responsibility with it. "The laws of nature tell us that if you've got it and you flaunt it, you'll lose it. But if you've been given a gift and you share it with those in need, it will multiply."

Psychologist Dr. Andrea Corn addresses the issue of celebrity and leadership from a different vantage point. "Perhaps this question could be slightly changed. What comes to mind are particular artists who were controversial, such as folk singer Bob Dylan or comedian Lenny Bruce. They were regarded as leaders in pop culture, but in fact, they represented the counterculture, or antiestablishment. I also think about the Beatles and how they revolutionized music. They were inspired and influenced by the times in which they lived, transforming an entire generation."

Andrea wonders whether performing artists are even interested in being seen as leaders, thinking of such unique and talented individuals as Madonna, Britney Spears, Taylor Swift, Beyonce, and others. "Yet when you see a celebrity such as Brad Pitt go to New Orleans to help rebuild the city following Hurricane Katrina, it can be very touching to see artists give back, helping to improve the infrastructure of the area or making a difference in the lives of those with far less."

HELPING OTHERS

Ingrid Hoffman believes in the power of "celebrity" in accomplishing goals to help others. "I don't like the word 'celebrity,' but I am someone who works in media and am a public person. Therefore, I've been able to bring attention to several causes in ways that someone that is not in the media may have difficulty in doing." In Ingrid's case, she engaged her sponsors and endorsers to help her create and sponsor public service announcements that have aired on national television to drive awareness to her various charitable endeavors and foundations, such as the New York City Food and Finance High School and Amigos for Kids. "We have successfully created not just awareness, but have raised funds through our national campaign. Working on this level always helps attract more money and volunteers."

And comedianne Sommore is particularly interested in celebrity and leadership. "As the question pertains to me as a stand-up comedianne, I notice that in America we glamorize the lifestyle and status of the celebrity and therefore have given them privileges that are not afforded others. Therefore, I feel that celebrities have an obligation to use their celebrity for the betterment of worthy causes."

INSTANT REPLAY

Artistic leadership and celebrity are powerful partners, finding audiences everywhere. Your celebrity as an artist can permit you to lend great weight to issues and causes you believe in.

THE POLITICS OF YOUR ART AND THE ART OF YOUR POLITICS

Your art makes a statement to the world and defines you as an artist and talent. But though understanding your art is one thing, understanding the nuances of politics is another.

Politics can define you as an individual and artist and may even define your work. And in the entertainment industry, one's politics can be expressed in a very potent and far-reaching fashion. If you are emerging within your field and are beginning to establish yourself as someone of prominence, you will invariably be caught up in a discussion of politics. That is expected and is very much part of our national consciousness.

People within the industry take their politics very seriously. Many individuals in front of or behind the camera have their charitable and educational causes, but they also have causes inextricably tied to politics.

So what of the artist's role as a celebrity engaged in politics in the entertainment industry? Emily Graham suggests this. "That begs the larger question. Is there an art to politics in the industry, and what is it? This is a personal issue for each celebrity. Some don't care about politics within the industry and don't have to worry about it too much because of their celebrity status. However, the industry is based on personal relationships and reputation, and to many people, political affiliations are as important as personal ones."

POLITICS IN THE INDUSTRY

Entertainment attorney Kim Kolback addresses the issue of politics in the entertainment industry and the positions one takes. "It depends whether the artist wants to be famous or infamous. Many comedians and urban artists have thrived on being 'politically incorrect,' such as Bill Maher. Interestingly, a 'politically correct' artist can inadvertently boost a lagging career by an inappropriate or unpopular statement, followed by an appropriate retraction or apology, of course."

Our belief in freedom of speech and other rights that we uphold as citizens permits us to speak freely about ourselves, our lives, our society, and our elected and appointed leaders.

However, as a successful artist, you are no longer just a person expressing an opinion. You are now a celebrity. Your words carry great weight, are very significant, and will be heard by many people around the world.

Remember, you will be judged not only by your political knowledge and savvy, but also by your ability to articulate your position. In other words, you must be intellectually prepared to defend your position on any given topic at hand, crystallizing the issues that are the subject of discussion and speaking in a logical and cogent manner.

Entertainment attorney Dixon Dern talks of politics and political correctness in the industry. "I think that artists, like everyone else, should be politically active, at least to the extent of caring about issues and expressing views when appropriate." Dixon also speaks about endorsements for candidates and issues. "Should well-known actors endorse candidates or issues? My personal belief is that they have as much right to do so as anyone else. The true import of this question is to ask whether they will be punished if active in politics. That is, will a Republican boss punish a Democrat employee, or the reverse? Certainly, in the old studio boss days, this was undoubtedly true, but today I don't think it is."

COMPROMISING YOUR BELIEFS

Should you compromise your political beliefs as a celebrity within the industry?

You should stand behind your beliefs rather than adopt a political position different from the one you believe in. Under our Constitution and democratic form of government, you have an absolute right to your position and the right to defend it, as well as the privilege of listening to others and giving them the opportunity to express themselves. The grand significance of all this is to demonstrate to your current and future colleagues and business partners that you are able to articulate your position with clarity and grace and at least listen to the positions of others, even if you disagree with them.

You will find that the world of successful professionals within your industry does not comprise a particularly large circle, and that most of the players know each other. They often find themselves either working together as allies or competing with each other as respectful adversaries. If there are political differences among them, these colleagues will in all likelihood not permit such ideological differences to affect their capacity to represent their interests or clients in a professional manner. You should always do the same.

In sum, your capacity to understand all sides of a political issue will be critical to the respect that you will command among your peers, and you will be regarded as a bright and articulate individual who has the capacity to listen to the viewpoints of others within the industry.

> **INSTANT REPLAY**
>
> Politics in the entertainment industry is generally issue oriented. Be true to yourself and your politics while understanding and respecting the rights of others to express different beliefs.

YOUR CIRCLES WITHIN THE INDUSTRY

In the industry, it is generally true that we maintain our friendships during the course of our professional careers. It will be these friendships that may remain with you for a lifetime. And all good friends can share contacts and other opportunities that may have a significant impact on your future.

What types of circles should you keep in the industry prior to and after success?

Emily Graham speaks of the importance of the right circles, commenting, "This depends on the personal circle and relationships around a client and the client's reputation. It should be noted that reputation can be a zero-sum game in Hollywood. Celebrities should not forget that they are professionals. Not only must they maintain a reputation for selling at the box office, but also for reliability and dependability."

KEEPING DOORS OPEN

Ingrid Hoffman feels that the personal and professional contacts and relationships within one's field can be instrumental to success, stating, "Yes, most definitely, they are very important. And it is important to always keep doors open. Most of these people I met years before, when they were guests at my restaurant and store, were people with whom I built great relationships, never knowing that I would work with them years later."

Miami television producer Elizabeth Angulo believes in becoming involved in the community in which one lives. She comments, "Whether you meet writers, below-the-line crew, agents, or anyone involved in your area of the industry, you are spending time and sharing ideas with people who want to give of their time to also meet others, to learn, and to expand their horizons. True friendships are forged by common interests. This way, you will develop a circle of friends who will remain with you for years. So be truthful to yourself and seek out like-minded people."

INSTANT REPLAY

It is your interest in the arts, society, and people in general that can help to drive your success as an artist. Relationships are important within the industry and can have a significant impact on your future and provide future opportunities.

CELEBRITY ETIQUETTE

Celebrity etiquette in the world of entertainment is also an important ingredient in success.

Earlier, etiquette expert Celeste Jones addressed the need for etiquette when one is being introduced to the industry. Now Celeste revisits that issue and the need for the artist to prepare for social graces that may be significant in the advanced development of a career. "Etiquette is often misconstrued as an antiquated aspect of business. However, etiquette today is better understood as conduct, which is of vital importance to anyone's career. Conduct represents the way individuals handle themselves in a variety of situations with diverse people and under many circumstances."

PEOPLE SKILLS

Celeste Jones explains that such skills, commonly known as "people skills," can make or break a person's professional advancement. Artists are public figures and must "be very careful about their image and about how they present themselves to everyone from the bellman to the housekeeper to the media, fans or potential clients. While people skills are a learned trait and some people are more adept at learning them than others, one should consider hiring a professional specializing in image and career development, such as an etiquette expert, to enhance these skills. Remember, the entertainment industry is so competitive that any edge over the competition helps."

Your circle of friends and colleagues should continue to expand as you embark upon your career and develop your name and reputation. The more you can do that, the greater the chance that opportunities will come your way.

> **INSTANT REPLAY**
>
> Celebrity etiquette, also thought of as people skills, involves your social conduct within the industry. This can also define you as a force in the world of entertainment.

EDUCATION AND MENTORING

Within the entertainment industry, the common wisdom is that as you begin your career, you should seek out the experience and wisdom of those who are knowledgeable with the system and who can educate you so that you will have the best chance for success. Similarly, as you find success within the industry, you will in turn be expected to help others who are just starting their careers.

This is educational outreach and mentoring.

THE RESPONSIBILITY OF GIVING BACK

Atlanta entertainment attorney Darryl Cohen has always been involved in education and mentoring through his efforts in continuing legal education. "Young artists are like clay. An emerging artist, regardless of his or her talent, starts out with no particular shape within the industry. That artist must be molded in such a way that his or her art is superb and has a nationally recognized market."

Emily Graham agrees. "Education and mentoring are especially important for an artist when tied to publicity on a national or international level." Entertainment attorney Tim Warnock states, "From a risk-management perspective, education and mentoring are extremely important, particularly for the artist who has little if any legal training." Author Carolina Garcia-Aguilera feels that most successful artists should be involved in mentoring and giving back as much as possible.

Dixon Dern believes in giving back. "Sure, it's good to give back, and I think that a lot of the established artists in the industry do give back and mentor, certainly in making films and the like. I have primarily seen this role performed by well-known artists. As to responsibility, I think the responsibility is no greater in our industry than any other. But we do need mentoring and training in order to bring on the next generation."

Entertainment attorney and author Todd Brabec also comments on this. "In the best of all possible worlds, you always give back. That assumes, of course, you recognize everything that was given to you which helped you to be the success you are. The choice in most cases is whether you give back quietly or actively. There is a responsibility attached to success, and that responsibility includes giving back."

Author and basketball coach Mike Jarvis speaks of education and mentoring in the world of sports. "To me, mentoring from the standpoint of the student has to do with understanding his or her role model and copying and imitating that role model. That is, we learn most of what we know from other people and particularly from those we respect and admire. So it is particularly admirable that a successful individual in the industry provide that type of assistance."

Musician and vocalist David Brigati provides an interesting insight when he remarks, "Remember, we are learned and accomplished artists and we are passing our knowledge on to other people."

The mentoring process never stops. It is perennial and eternal.

MENTORING OTHERS

Ingrid Hoffman discusses mentoring and its importance in the process. "I was mentored at the beginning of my career by some wonderful people, including Mr. Luis Balaguer of Latin World Entertainment, who has made many stars in the industry." Ingrid stated that Luis showed her the ropes, believing she was a quick study. She also received a lot of advice from her sister, Johanna Hoffman, who handled public relations for Martha Stewart, as well as Nahyr Acosta, her editor at *Buen Hogar* magazine, and her first producer, Julia Dangond.

Artistic director Diana Lozano has mentored many performers who either work with her or are students of hers. "Currently, I am a teacher at the New World School of the Arts in Miami. I feel blessed to be able to teach improvisation and self-expression to teens, ages 14 through 16. Clearly, I remember being at that age, and how frustrating and isolating it was to not have the adults understand what I was going through or the kind of work I wanted to create. Now I have the chance to be an inspiration to other teens." Diana notes that most of the children she teaches cannot wait until they graduate so that they can move into the world of creative art.

Steve Alten understands the importance of education and mentoring and has instituted a program designed for them. "Adopt-an-Author is a nationwide nonprofit teen reading program I started 10 years ago when I became inundated with middle and high school students' emails, all telling me they hated to read until they read my novel *Meg*. After *Meg* was named a top book for young adult readers, even though it is adult fiction, I created the program, which combines free curriculum materials, posters, and other materials including direct contact with myself and other authors. We now have over 10,000 registered teachers and have been called the best secondary school reading program in existence today. And it's all free, paid by me and our sponsors."

Your involvement in education and mentoring may be one of the most relevant things you can do as an artist. Just ask other artists who have done it and they will tell you how rewarding it truly is.

BECOMING A ROLE MODEL

As a mentor, how important is it to become a role model?

Dr. Andrea Corn emphasizes its importance. "Perhaps mentors who are older and wiser can be supportive, empathic, and serve as role models for younger artists. By teaching self-acceptance to the artist while he or she hones a craft, one may also be holding on to, and not letting go of, one's vision for the future."

Andrea also explains that, depending on the artist, some may even turn to mentors in spiritual or religious teachings for inspiration to maintain a positive focus in order to avoid losing sight of the ultimate goal. "Developing willpower is also important since without it, many artists may begin to feel defeated, not realizing that it is not the time to give up, but to persevere through difficult times."

Regardless of the direction you choose, being involved in education and mentoring is also a vital part of the social process today. From a practical standpoint, this will permit you to expand your level of contacts within the entertainment industry, bringing you full circle in your chosen industry at relatively high levels, and perhaps inviting more business and professional opportunities in your field.

ORGANIZATIONS IN SUPPORT OF EDUCATION AND MENTORING

Practically everyone who wishes to be successful in the industry takes part in some way in the continuing educational process once success begins to happen.

For example, in Los Angeles, programs and classes in education and mentoring are found within the university community, professional organizations, or community and charitable entities. There are continuing education programs at the University of California, Los Angeles (UCLA), the University of Southern California (USC), and Loyola Marymount University, as well as other schools in the area.

Most state, local, and voluntary bar associations in the country promote mentoring and continuing legal education for lawyers and industry professionals, including courses covering the world of entertainment law and intellectual property. In this manner, lawyers are able to remain knowledgeable within their respective fields of law and are thus better prepared to represent their clients effectively and professionally.

As an artist and industry professional, you are, for the most part, welcome to attend such seminars and programs for a fee that is generally less expensive than what lawyers are charged. And this is an excellent way to broaden your business horizons and better understand today's issues in entertainment law.

These programs or courses, most of which are conducted in the early evening to attract students who may work during the day, are taught by adjunct professors, who are also professionals giving their time to teach others the knowledge needed for success in their respective industries. In Los Angeles, there are also continuing legal education programs at the UCLA School of Law, the USC

Gould School of Law, Southwestern Law School, and other area law schools.

Additionally, there are continuing education programs and seminars offered by professional organizations such as the Recording Academy (the Academy of Recording Arts and Sciences), the Television Academy (the Academy of Television Arts and Sciences), the Motion Picture Academy (the Academy of Motion Picture Arts and Sciences), and Women in Film (WIF).

Whether you attend continuing education courses or take part in their instruction, it will be beneficial to do so in order to maintain your presence in education circles. This will permit you to continue to establish your reputation in the industry as one who believes in education and its ability to empower, and who wishes to help others and give back to the arts community.

Your decision to become involved in education and mentoring, as a student or lecturer, can be an integral part of your plan to further develop your reputation as one who graciously shares time and knowledge with others in the industry.

In fact, it is expected of you once you begin to find success.

INSTANT REPLAY

Education and mentoring permit you to help others who may find your experience and expertise invaluable as they begin their careers within the industry. This also entitles you to give back to your community and your profession, allowing you to become a role model to your peers and those emerging artists within the industry.

CHARITABLE AND CIVIC INVOLVEMENT

It is generally recognized that anyone who has found success should be involved with and supportive of charitable causes and civic organizations. Aside from the obvious benefit to the organization, a byproduct of such involvement is that the artist is regarded as one who gives back to the community.

In fact, within the entertainment industry, as in other industries, there are those who work tirelessly to provide assistance to a particular charity or are involved in civic organizations. Such assistance and involvement are very personal to the individual. And it is important to provide assistance to others. One should not tie it to a professional or business goal. It is simply something that demonstrates your commitment to humanity.

THE IMPORTANCE OF INVOLVEMENT

How important is involvement in charitable and civic affairs? Should an artist provide charitable and other assistance to his or her community?

Darryl Cohen states, "The more the talent is involved in his or her community, both on a charitable and civic basis, the better it is. No one can underestimate the value of that type of valuable publicity. But most importantly, it's the right thing to do." Theatrical producer Frannie Sheridan agrees, citing her own experiences. "My way of being philanthropic is to perform at fundraisers. In this manner, I can help. Recently, I have had the opportunity to give back by performing at fundraisers at various venues, such as for the Women's International Zionist Organization and the Montreal Jewish General Hospital."

Coach Mike Jarvis feels involvement in such causes is critical. "Charitable and civic causes teach young people to be successful and do the right things, to love our neighbors as ourselves, and to take our special gifts and share them with other people. To have things and not share them with others is wrong." Emily Graham states, "Charitable and civic involvement is essential in order to elevate and maintain 'star' power. But basically, it is the right thing to do and puts the charitable or civic cause in the spotlight."

And Celeste Jones feels that charitable involvement is critical to the artist. "It is very important to give back to the universe. We live in a reflection of what we put out or give to the world and it all comes back to us. So artists who are nice to everyone, down to earth, and philanthropic will have this goodness come back to them in their own lives."

VOLUNTEERISM

René Katz believes in the concept of volunteerism in civic affairs in the world of entertainment and particularly for charities. "Usually, one has a connection to a particular charity or a conviction and belief that it is appropriate to be involved in these kinds of activities. Always remember that your beliefs and convictions should be the predominant reason to be involved and to help others."

Entertainment attorney Henry Root notes, "I believe that all of us have a moral imperative to contribute to our communities, to engage in philanthropic activities, and to do so from a sense of selflessness and charity and not from a sense of, or with the goal of, personal aggrandizement or career enhancement."

Henry cites an example in the music industry. "One way to help is by participating in live, in-concert fundraisers and awareness campaigns, such as Stand Up to Cancer, Farm Aid, The Concert for 9-11, and others. You might notice that typically the names of the artists who participate and the others involved in the production are not credited on screen or in the end-title credit scroll. That is because participation in community activities, philanthropic endeavors, and social-cause awareness should be done from the goodness of the artist's heart."

Television personality and spokesperson Jenna Edwards is no stranger to charitable causes, firmly believing in the importance of giving back. Jenna made her charity, the For a Day Foundation, one of the centerpieces of her career in the industry, and she always speaks about the importance of the charity and of charitable involvement. And Dr. James Huysman notes that artists "must understand their goal so they realize that this may not bring money or exposure. And while it may enhance their celebrity, the true reason to engage in charity is to be charitable."

Most artists involved in charitable and civic matters find that they will establish long-standing relationships with other successful artists who donate their time and money to their particular charities. That should apply to you as well. By contributing in a selfless manner, you will be recognized by your colleagues within the industry for your charitable and civic efforts, regardless of the form that commitment may take. Most important, you should be charitable and help others because it is the right thing to do.

> **INSTANT REPLAY**
>
> Charitable and civic involvement constitutes another method of giving back to your community. This type of participation also gives you the opportunity to establish yourself and help others who wish to follow in your path.

DEFINING SUCCESS

What is it that truly defines success?

Is it simply a tag that attaches to an individual who is the subject of accolades in his or her chosen profession? Is it a title we bestow upon a person who reaches the pinnacle of success in a particular field or endeavor? Or is it more than that?

SUCCESS HAS A MEANING

Producer Maryann Ridini Spencer speaks of what success means to her. "If you are passionate about the story or project and its message, you will find that there can be many people between you and completion of that story or project that can influence the outcome of what is actually seen on screen. So when you watch your work come to fruition on the screen as you hoped and envisioned, you have found success and fulfillment beyond measure."

Television personality and gallerist Adriana De Moura states, "You must be strong and sure of yourself in order to survive, since once you become a known personality, you are under a microscope. And you must be resilient and kind to yourself when it comes to criticism directed at you. Please do not take it, or yourself, too seriously." Robin Abramovitz Goldberg comments, "If we look at the attempt to become successful and the reality of success achieved, we must be honest with ourselves. For me, the attempt itself is just as thrilling and rewarding as the success. It is a journey unto itself and constitutes its own reality."

Darryl Cohen often advises his clients on what needs to be done in order to continue to achieve success. "Give as much as you can to your art! Give them more than anyone would expect. Then maybe, just maybe, you will have a chance to find success within the industry." Jenna Edwards defines success as finding that project that makes it all worthwhile. "I always look for longevity in a project. At this point in my career, I want to create relationships that permit me to grow and evolve. The broader vision is to develop a brand and a following so I can promote my philanthropic pursuits on a grander scale. I believe my entertainment career is a stepping stone towards influencing community and government for worthwhile causes."

A STRONG SENSE OF IDENTITY

Henry Root has this advice. "My words of wisdom are the same for all my clients, regardless of their degree of success attained: be guided by your instincts. The most successful artists are those who have a strong sense of identity and know where they want to be as well as who they aspire to be. If the artist has a strong sense of personal identity and vision and makes decisions based on instinct, they will never second-guess themselves."

And Coach Mike Jarvis states, "Success is when you can go to bed at night knowing that you used your gifts to the best of your abilities so you can become the finest that you can be. It is about the journey. And in sports, when you lose a game, it does not mean you have lost in life or were not successful. But remember that it is what you do when you lose that determines how successful you really are. I tell my players that the only time you lose in anything is when you do not learn from your experience."

Success can be a state of mind and will vary depending on the individual. So enjoy and appreciate your art and all that you are as an artist. And continue to develop your art so all the world may enjoy it.

INSTANT REPLAY

Success within your art begins and ends with what lives inside of you and your perception of it. Only you can define success. Simply follow your art and you will find success.

AND IT'S A WRAP

And it's a wrap, with some thoughts for your consideration.

Understand the importance of maintaining artistic leadership among your peers and colleagues in the entertainment industry.

Realize the power of celebrity as well as its significance and the goodwill it may bring. This is especially true given that once you are regarded as successful in your field, it will be necessary to exercise great care in all that you do or say. Your celebrity status is equivalent to great power, and you must exercise that power with poise, care, and grace, as celebrity and leadership merge.

Be cognizant of the world of politics in the entertainment industry and consider not only the politics of your artistry as a mode of expression, but also the politics of your actions and the issues you wish to address as an artist and concerned citizen. Stay involved and remain a part of the process, realizing that such a responsibility is universal, regardless of your profession.

Know your circles in the new entertainment industry. Understand the vital importance of continuing education and the mentoring process for emerging artists, as well as charitable and civic involvement, which are part of your responsibility to give back to your community.

FILM

★ As a rising star in the motion picture industry, you have the opportunity to demonstrate leadership and act as a role model to others while further enhancing your reputation as a gifted individual and artist.

★ Your role outside the industry is just as important and includes your involvement in leadership, education, mentoring, and charitable and civic causes. Within this industry, such activities will gain you a great deal of respect and the accolades of your colleagues.

TELEVISION

★ As in film, the television industry is composed of many people who care about others and who want to help in education, mentoring, and charitable and civic affairs.

★ These efforts are woven into the fabric of the industry.

MUSIC

★ Be involved in charity and giving. It is absolutely a part of the music industry and always has been.

THE LITERARY ARTS

★ Make your best efforts to be involved in education, mentoring, and charitable and civic affairs. As a writer, you are a person of letters and a leader, and those around you will look to you for your leadership.

★ Writers can be a reader's window to the world. Share with your readers not only your writings but also your belief in the goodness that can be done to help others.

FASHION AND MODELING

★ The fashion and modeling industries have always been supportive of causes.

★ Be giving of your time and charitable to those who need it. The world will appreciate your work in the industry and will admire you not just for your talents and gifts, but also for your philanthropy.

THE VISUAL ARTS AND THE FINE ARTS

★ Demonstrate your commitment to the visual arts and fine arts by supporting education, mentoring, and civic and charitable causes, and donate your time to such worthy causes.

TEAM HUDDLE

Now that you have arrived, the real work begins, as you continue to coordinate with your entire team to further develop the direction of your career and leave your artistic mark on the new entertainment industry. Leadership in the industry will define you as an individual as well as an artist.

★ Your entertainment attorney may tell you that although hard work is part of the path to success, harder work will keep you there. This is especially true in the entertainment industry.

★ Your talent manager will continue to look for the best artistic opportunities that may arise and bring them to your attention as your reputation grows.

★ Your literary manager and writing coach will assist you in honing your skills in your craft by providing advice on the projects you may become involved in.

★ Your agent will also look for business opportunities that bring you greater exposure as an artist.

★ Your editor will be available to help you from a literary standpoint, always coordinating with your literary manager.

★ Your producer will continue to look for ways to present your projects in the most professional, artistic manner.

★ Your publicist will be there to promote you in times of your successes and work with you as your career reaches new heights.

LIGHTS, CAMERA, ACTION!

You have the ability to leave an artistic legacy as you continue to create great art and reach higher goals, helping other artists in the process. With your team and your entertainment attorney in the lead, you should strive for all that you can achieve. The future will hold great promise for you.

A STORY INSPIRED BY A COMPOSER AND THE PERFECT PERFORMANCE

The tropical Miami sun had set, and evening was descending on South Florida.

The composer and pianist stood on the balcony of his hotel and admired the view of Biscayne Bay and Miami Beach. He had traveled around the world, yet felt a particular sense of belonging whenever he traveled here to perform.

He had flown in from New York City the night before, having been asked to appear at a special pre-Super Bowl concert gala at the new Adrienne Arsht Center for the Performing Arts in downtown Miami.

A Steinway artist, he was regarded as an acclaimed composer in classical crossover music, having created and performed numerous internationally known symphonic and other pieces, including his masterpiece, *The Holocaust Symphony*, which had been performed around the world.

His works had been performed with leading symphonies in the United States, London, Moscow, St. Petersburg, and Beijing.

The drive to the Arsht Center took him through the streets of Miami, lit up for Super Bowl weekend. Everywhere he looked, he saw color, texture, and movement. Miami was a city of light, appearing to rise out of the ocean, gleaming with white buildings and pastel colors. It lived up to its reputation as the magic city.

He arrived at the concert hall and strolled backstage to prepare for his performance.

Inside the performing arts center was a full house of over two thousand people, boisterous and in holiday spirits, having arrived in Miami to attend the Super Bowl and hear some great music.

His performance time grew closer. The minutes seemed to never end as he stood at stage right, waiting to be introduced.

His mental preparations continued. While waiting, he looked at the Steinway piano at center stage and glanced at the audience. He folded his hands and appeared as if he were meditating. Those around him wished him the best of luck, but he did not really seem to hear them, wanting to maintain his concentration.

He had decided some time ago that he would perform a movement from his Adagio for Piano and Orchestra.

He entered. When he appeared, silence filled the room and he was greeted with polite but strong applause.

He lifted his jacket and sat at the piano.

He did not need sheet music, having memorized this piece years before.

A moment passed. The cavernous auditorium was silent as the audience waited for the performance.

He began to play.

The introduction to the piece was dazzling. It was as if his fingers simply touched the keys, speaking to them as they spoke back.

The audience sat in silence and listened.

The movement reached a crescendo as the auditorium filled with music. He had been performing for eight minutes.

The adagio was beautiful. When he played the final note, the audience exploded into applause, giving him a standing ovation.

"Bravo! Bravo, Maestro," they shouted and whistled.

He stood, smiled, and bowed.

It was the perfect performance on a perfect evening in Miami.

The performer was an acclaimed international classical crossover composer.

He was the late, great Richard Nanes.

And he was an artist.

ENCORE

THE SPIRIT OF SUCCESS
AND YOUR CREATIVE STAR

When I was a boy, my guitar was my joy
And oh, Lord, how I'd play and I'd sing
About soldiers and ships and of far away trips
And of finding the girl of my dreams.

Richard Warren Rappaport, "Magic Man,"
from the motion picture soundtrack of *Concert*

SUCCESS AND YOUR CREATIVE STAR

Success lives within our spirit and exists as a part of us. For some, it is the attempt that defines success. For others, it is the journey. But for many artists, it is sharing an artistic gift with the world.

The stories that have followed each chapter deal with artists like you who worked very hard to achieve success within the entertainment industry.

But let's end where we began: with you, the artist.

You are the one best equipped, artistically and intellectually, to create your art. Beyond your art, all that is needed is your ongoing and unequivocal commitment to finding success.

Life teaches us that there is no such thing as an end to our accomplishments. There are always new beginnings, new goals to accomplish, and new horizons to reach.

It is your choice to determine what level of success you desire to achieve. Once you reach that level, you can decide whether or not you wish to continue. From an artistic standpoint, the choice is entirely yours.

So be confident, focused, and energetic. Be true to your art. Be true to yourself. And be giving to others once you achieve success so that you may share your experiences with them in order that they may also find success.

As stated in the prelude to this book, artistry has a beginning. But it never really has an end. It is true and speaks of the dynamic and artistic nature of creativity and its importance to the arts and the world.

You are the artist. Reach for your creative star.

—*Richard Warren Rappaport*

INDEX